Sound and Look Professional on Television and the Internet

How to Improve Your On-Camera Presence

Michelle McCoy
with
Ann S. Utterback, Ph.D.

Bonus Books, Inc., Chicago

Credits

Contributing Writers
* David Marc McCoy, Kent State University
* Dawn Waldrop, Best Impressions, Inc.
* David Cupp, News Director, WVIR-TV
* Olga Morales, National Make-Up Artist

Senior Copy Editor
Stanley T. Wearden, Ph.D.

Copy Editors
Craig Urey
Terry Sosnowski, Ph.D.

Format
Judy Smith

Reviewers
Gary Hanson
Charles Richie

Front Cover Design
Jim Hurguy

Graphics
Diane Sperko
Renee Garlock

The eyeglass graphic in Chapter 4 is reprinted with permission from Barbizon International.

04   03   02   01   00   5   4   3   2   1

Library of Congress Control Number: 00-107293

ISBN: 1-56625-154-0

Bonus Books
160 East Illinois Street
Chicago, Illinois 60611

Printed in the United States of America

Contents

Acknowledgments   ix

Foreword   xi

1   So, You're Going to Be On Camera   1

ON-CAMERA OPPORTUNITIES

2   Broadcast Production Studios   7
     Microphones and Their Uses   8
     TelePrompTers   10
     Studio Cues   11
     Role of the Floor Director   13

Microphone Dressing and Audio Checks 13
Production Assistants 17

3 **News Anchors and Reporters** 21
On-Air Positions 22
The Reporter 22
   Preparation 22
   Live Shots 24
   Talking Points 24
   Movement and Reporters 25
   Writing 25
The Anchor 25
   Movement and Anchors 26
   TelePrompTers 26
   Stance 27
   Spontaneity 27

4 **Talk Shows: Appearing as the Host** 31
Topics 31
Finding Guests 32
Fact Gathering 33
Question Guides 34
Structuring Questions 35
Settings 38
Warm-Ups 39
Call-In Shows 39
Demonstrations 40

5 **Talk Shows: Appearing as a Guest** 43
The Booking 43
Appearance 44
Research 45
The Set 46
Preparation 47
Show Time 48

6 **On-Camera Commercials** 51
Character Types 53
Auditions 54

Preparation 54
Marks and Props 55
Products 55
Typical Shooting Day 56
Voice-Overs 57
Timing 58
Donuts 59

7 **Industrial Videos** 63
The Product 64
Environment 65
Ear Assist 65
Content and Delivery 67
Character 68
Auditions 68
Clothing 72
Teleconference and Distance Learning 73
The Internet 73

8 **Film and TV Acting** 77
Technique 77
Actor's Profile 79
Stage vs. TV and Film 80
Script Analysis 81
Sides 82
Memorization, Listening and Reacting 82
Blocking and Movement 84
Props 85
Maintaining Energy 85

ON-CAMERA TOOLBOX

9 **On-Camera Makeup** 91
Supplies 92
Makeup and Lighting 98
Shopping 99

People of Color 100
Aging and Cosmetic Surgery 101

10 Hairstyles for TV 107
The Look 107
Facial Shape 108
Styles 109
Hair Textures and Products 109
Consultations 110
Nails 111

11 Wardrobe for TV 113
Style 114
Natural 114
Classic 115
Romantic 115
Dramatic 116
Things to Remember 117
Colors 118
Backdrops 119
Fabrics and Textures 119
Good Fabric Choices 121
Accessories 122
Accessory List 122
Shopping 128
Alterations 129

12 Broadcast Voice 131
Breathing 132
Phonation 136
Vocal Health 136
Resonanace 139
Articulation 140

13 Sounding Conversational 143
Script Marking 144
Meaning-Laden Words 147

Talking to a Person 149
    Visualization 149
Emotion 150

14   **Tips for Business** 155
Marketing Yourself 155
Resumes 156
Cover Letters 156
    Sending Yourself Through the Mail
    to a News Director 159
    How to Get Started 164
Agents 167
    Agencies 168
Contracts 169
Unions 170
Photos 170
Demo Tapes 171
    Success Formula 172
Audition Tips for Commercial Television 174
Interview and Audition Tips for News 175

Notes 179

Glossary 183

Suggested Reading and Information 195

Index 197

ACKNOWLEDGMENTS

The creation of this book was a team effort. First, I want to thank Ann S. Utterback for her constant motivation—she has been a wonderful mentor. Also, the director of Kent State University's School of Journalism and Mass Communication, Pam Creedon, has been a constant support. The following people have provided me with guidance in various capacities: Stan Wearden, Timothy Smith, Roger Fidler, Zoe Macatharin, Gary Hanson, Charles Richie, Terry Sosnowski, Grace Luthy, Devon Freeny, LuEtt Hanson, Rohn Thomas, Mark LaMura, Karen Fields, Karen Sheets, Craig Urey, Jan Jones, J. Sheldon Artz, Diane Sperko, Renee Garlock, Jim Hurguy, Timothy McCoy, Kelly Olexia, Mary Cusick, Barry Wolff, Thomas Olson, Vickie Lynn, Gordon J. Murray and Judy Smith (for keeping things organized). In addition, I want to recognize all my friends at AAUW for their continual enthusiasm and Molly Merryman, along with my contributing writers, Dawn Waldrop, Dave Cupp, Olga Morales and my husband, Dave, for his contributions and relentless encouragement. This book is dedicated to my mother—my inspiration.

Michelle McCoy
Kent State University, Stark Campus, Ohio

My greatest teachers over the past fifteen years have been my clients, who have come to me from every aspect of television news as well as the worlds of business and politics. These clients have guided me in broadening my professional expertise to meet their needs. I am very grateful to them all. I also owe a debt to many news directors and bureau chiefs who have supported my work along the way. Many of these clients and managers have become friends, which has been an unexpected pleasure. I send special thanks to them for their friendship and support. And, as always, my most heartfelt appreciation goes to my husband, Jim, who continues to be my best critic and strongest support.

Ann S. Utterback, Ph.D.
Washington, D.C.

FOREWORD

"Just be yourself . . . ." The worst three words a person can hear just before going on television. How can you possibly be yourself with bright, hot lights in your face, people standing silently in the studio watching and listening to your every word, and the camera recording your every expression? How can you possibly be yourself in such artificial circumstances? After years spent on television as an actress, early in my career, and then as a news anchor at small market stations and, eventually, at the network level, this is a question I have faced daily. What I have learned is if you can control some elements, such as your appearance and voice, you can relax and let who you are shine through the camera.

Having, in my career, traversed from acting to television news, I can tell you that the same skills will help you excel in both fields. The more tools you can use to help you relax and show your true self, the better. Bringing yourself to the job is what will separate you from your competitors. This is an ongoing process that you will continue throughout your career, and this book is an excellent launching pad.

I am honored to write the foreword for *Sound and Look Professional on Television and the Internet* because I know there are no better professionals to write this book than Dr. Ann S. Utterback and Michelle McCoy. Ann has been a friend and coach of mine for almost 10 years. She has trained hundreds of the top news broadcasters in the United States and around the world. Members of Congress, political candidates, and corporate executives also call on Ann for media training. Michelle McCoy not only teaches beginning broadcasters, but she works in the business as well. She hosts talk shows, appears in television commercials, and does voice-over work. The experience of these women could certainly fill more than one book! Trust what they say.

With the knowledge you will gain from *Sound and Look Professional on Television and the Internet*, the next time you are about to go on television and the director looks at you and says, "Just be yourself," you can smile calmly and let your own magic shine!

—Page Hopkins
Anchor
Bloomberg Television News

SO, YOU'RE GOING TO BE ON CAMERA

In the digital communication age, opportunities are becoming endless for professional talent, along with everyone else, to perform in front of cameras either on television or the Internet. This is partially due to the pervasiveness of the media and the increasing use of new technologies. Senior executives of companies, for example, are now often called upon to create audio and video segments for websites and CD-ROMs. It is not uncommon for a CEO to participate in a teleconference, a television or radio press conference, and a radio or television talk show all in one day! Roger Fidler, author and new media pioneer, has remarked, "In the digital age, everyone has the potential of becoming a performer on a virtual stage."[1]

One aspect that is often overlooked with Internet broadcasting is that it is being compared to the best television broadcasts. Because the Internet carries all forms of video, the comparison is inevitable (see Figure 1). If Internet video is being used for business purposes, it needs to look and sound professional because it will be compared with the most sophisticated television productions shown on the Internet. Professionals should not let Internet video hurt their credibility or the credibility of their company just because it is only being done for the Internet. Even a video e-mail needs to have a professional look and sound.

Executives representing their companies, or students aspiring to work in the broadcast field, are often intimidated by the thought of going on camera for television or the Internet. Many people are uncomfortable with how they may look in front of the camera, or uncomfortable with their voices. Mary Cusick, former president of the Public Relations Society of America (PRSA), and current vice president of Corporate Communications for Bob Evans Farms, says, "The more prepared executives are in front of the camera or a microphone, the more confident they become. . . . This ease with the process allows them to focus on the issues at hand instead of being concerned about lights, microphones, etc."

Figure I

Types of Internet Broadcasts

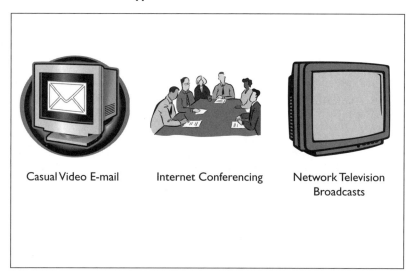

Casual Video E-mail   Internet Conferencing   Network Television
                                                          Broadcasts

Corporate executives are not alone in their fears. A professor once told us that he was frightened to death to lecture in front of a camera for a distance learning class. Without human feedback, he could not stop asking himself, "Am I doing a good job? How can I converse with a camera lens on a tripod?" Other acquaintances of ours, who are successful authors, are petrified of book tours because they will be required to appear on television or radio talk programs. They wonder, "What should I wear on television? What should I expect?" One of the reasons for these fears is that there are so few resources to aid in educating people about broadcast performing expectations.

Many television news directors and producers believe that recent college graduates, looking for their first jobs in the broadcasting industry, are not prepared for what to expect in the business either. They are unsure about television makeup application, wardrobe requirements, vocal inflections and resumes. Tim McCoy, general manager of an NBC television affiliate, says, "Rarely do I find job-seeking recent college graduates in broadcasting who have the same vision of TV anchors or reporters I do. It seems talent have to learn about performance tips on the job."

Whether you are a corporate executive or an aspiring reporter, *Sound and Look Professional on Television and the Internet* will help you prepare for any broadcasting experience. You will learn how your voice works as your most important tool in broadcasting, along with how to maintain a healthy sound through stress reduction and a healthy lifestyle. On-camera makeup application is covered in detail so that you can attempt the process on your own. You will find hairstyle and wardrobe advice that follows some general principles for people appearing on camera. In addition, this book provides studio basics, outlining the different requirements for broadcast news, corporate videos (industrials), the Internet, voice-overs, television acting, and marketing oneself. This book is a user-friendly reference tool for anyone faced with a visit to a television studio or a corporate video production house. Our best wishes to you in your broadcasting endeavors.

ON-CAMERA OPPORTUNITIES

☑ Broadcast Production Studios

☑ News Anchors/Reporters

☑ Talk Shows: Appearing as a Host

☑ Talk Shows: Appearing as a Guest

☑ On-Camera Commercials

☑ Industrial Videos

☑ Film/Television Acting

BROADCAST PRODUCTION STUDIOS

One of the first things you will want to know when you walk into a studio is who all the players are. To feel comfortable in front of the camera, it helps to know a little about the roles different staff have and what they do. Even if you are already in the business, it could be useful to review some of the roles of your associates. Many books describe the roles and responsibilities of the television production crew and the director, but few focus on working with talent in the studio.

The most important person you will work with is the producer who is in charge of the production. Producers are both idea and budget people as they organize the show, coordinate rehearsal schedules and pay the crew. Sometimes, producers are the first people you see when you get involved in a television program. They hire most of the crew, including talent, schedule auditions, rent facilities, purchase scripts and oversee editing sessions. Producers hire the director who will conduct rehearsals and direct the recording. On some occasions, producers also serve as the program's director. At this point, you will begin to work closely with the director.

Historically, the director worked in the studio environment and coordinated theatre-like live performances for broadcast. Today, many productions are taped in advance, allowing directors control of all the production aspects except for the performance of the talent. This type of director can be referred to as the *production director*. The other type of director fits an *aesthetic* model, working closely with the talent, like a theatre director, on blocking, delivery, gestures and other performance aspects.

Sometimes productions contain people who fit both roles. For example, a high-budget show might enlist a *performance director* who works exclusively in the studio, or at the remote site, with talent. Also, you may hear someone referred to as the *control room director*. This person functions as a coordinator of all behind-the-scenes elements. In this situation, you will deal mostly with the performance director and rarely with the control room director. Basically, the producer and the director are the core of the production; however, you also will meet other people who play important roles. We will introduce you to the rest of the production crew later in this chapter.

Microphones and Their Uses

In addition to knowing some of the people and their roles, you need to recognize the importance of audio during broadcast taping. The proper use of the microphone in a video production is an essential part of your understanding of the medium. Microphones come in many different sizes and shapes, but above all, they have different applications. As a broadcaster, you need to know the three most important types of microphones you will work with during a production, whether it be for television or the Internet, in a studio or at a remote location:

LAVALIER—a small microphone used to pick up individual voices. Usually attached to the person's clothing, and positioned close to the sound source.

HAND-HELD—a small, rugged microphone designed to be held by talent or positioned on a desk in a sound booth or on a news desk. Commonly, hand-held microphones are designed for use close to the sound source.

SHOTGUN—a large microphone designed to isolate a sound source. Shotguns are usually microphones that are operated on booms or fishpoles. They capture good sound without having to be extremely close to the sound source.

Shotgun microphones are used predominately during dramatic presentations like soap operas and at remote settings because they are flexible enough to pick up sounds of multiple people in environments where microphone cables should not be seen. They also are useful in a crowded situation, like an event in front of the White House where there would be many production crews and reporters.

Hand-held microphones usually are used for musical performances, interviews, studio recordings done in a sound booth (recording room) and recordings at remote settings ("lives"). They can be used by a single broadcaster or shared among two or more on-camera people. The correct use of a hand-held microphone is an art. The manner in which you hold the microphone expresses both your confidence in your performance and your experience in the television profession. A microphone head should not be held so high that it impedes the sound quality and visually blocks your mouth, nor should it be held so low as to make your voice sound faint or to distract the viewer's eyes from your face. *Generally, hand-held microphone heads should be 6 to 8 inches below the mouth and 4 to 5 inches away from the body.*

Correct gripping of the microphone allows for relaxed performances, good sound quality and limited visual distraction. Try not to hold your microphone too tightly, as it will not only cause a tense and rigid look, but it also will make the microphone shaft slippery from perspiration. Also, try to avoid holding the microphone with two hands—it looks bad and suggests that you are very nervous and unsure. The best method is to hold the microphone with your dominant hand (right hand for righties, left hand for lefties) and use the less dominant hand for natural gestures.

If you are doing a voice-over (audio recording only), you will probably find yourself recording in a sound booth. This recording area is usually sound-proof, probably has excellent acoustics and is usually equipped with a desk microphone on a stand or a gooseneck (a flexible metal extension to hold a microphone). You may wear a headset microphone so you can communicate and hear the director's cues.

Many talent get annoyed with the headset microphone because of the tendency to want to speak into that microphone instead of the desk microphone. In this situation, you can place the mouthpiece of the headset microphone under your chin, so that it is below your lips. Some sound booths have the equipment capabilities to allow you to stand when recording. Your vocal delivery will improve immensely when you stand (see Dr. Ann S. Utterback's *Broadcast Voice Handbook* for more details).

Whenever you will be moving around, a *wireless microphone*, with no visible cable attachments, is best. The wireless feature can be adapted to lavaliers, hand-held microphones and shotgun microphones. The important issue here is that wireless microphones make it easier for you to move.

TelePrompTers

Delivering lines or reading copy is difficult, especially if you must maintain eye contact with the camera. Historically, talent memorized lines, glanced at scripts or read from printed cue cards, but each of these methods had severe drawbacks. The solution to these problems was the ***TelePrompTer***. TelePrompTers are devices that project moving copy over the lens of the camera to ensure that the broadcasters maintain eye contact with the viewer. People who do on-air speeches, television news or entertainment, who are required to have some direct eye contact with the camera, use TelePrompTers. By using text generated from a computer program, TelePrompTers allow for ease of application and readability.

Electronic prompters are favored over cue cards by most professional talent. In addition to enabling direct eye contact, quick changes to the script are easier to make on the prompter keyboard than by finding and writing on the appropriate cardboard cue cards. You must keep in mind, however, your distance from the camera is very important with TelePrompTer use. If you are too close to the camera, then the movement of your eyes, as copy is read, becomes overly visible. Constant eye movement can be very distracting to a viewer.

Remember to rehearse prompter reads with the operator. While the operator mechanically controls the speed of the copy, your rate of speech and delivery will dictate how fast or slow the operator moves the prompter text. A rehearsal will allow the prompter operator to fluidly keep pace with your delivery and ensure little chance of mistakes during the actual production.

Studio Cues

In the studio setting, you will take direction from the *floor director*, whose responsibility calls for some visual commands that draw your attention to the action. The floor director stands near one of the cameras and signals to you with hand gestures. For you to be able to respond to a direct command or *cue*, you must be given ample preparation time to mentally ready yourself to perform. Therefore, a *standby* or *ready cue* is given to alert you and provide you with some time before action takes place. Generally, the standby cue is directed to everyone in the studio, while the ready cue is directed to the talent who will begin the sequence or program (see Figure 2).

Before the start of the program or when your microphone is off, the ready cue is an oral statement, such as "*Standby on one,*" or "*Ready on one.*" If the program already has commenced, or if your microphone is on, then the floor director will give a silent *ready cue*, which is an upraised hand (see Figure 2).

There are times where it is essential to switch your viewpoint to another camera. To allow for smooth transitions, you need to follow the floor director's cue or watch the *tally light* change. Tally lights are the red lights on the front of each camera which are illuminated when the picture from that camera is transmitted to the line monitor or over the air. The problem with relying solely upon the tally lights is that they give you no warning that a change is coming. For this reason, it is recommended that you watch the floor director out of the corner of your eye and follow his gesture.

During a camera change, the floor director will direct your attention from one camera to another. This maneuver is best described as a hand, near the on-air camera, sweeping in an underhanded arc pattern toward the newly selected camera. The performer will follow the downward pattern of the floor director's hand as it moves to the other camera.

Usually in an interview show, when your attention is focused on the guest, the floor director will give you cues. Good floor directors know *not* to cue you when the focus is on you. Instead he will wait until there is a close-up shot of the guest. This way, you can acknowledge his cues when you are off camera so your eyes are not wandering. If you are on a two shot (you and the guest), use your peripheral vision to notice the cues. You never want to look or be distracted when you are on camera.

Moreover, the experienced floor directors will enhance your performance by not giving signals or cues when you are speaking, as that can lead to confusion. They will wait until after you have completed your question or comment to give you commands.

Role of the Floor Director

As a performer, you need to understand that the floor director is the studio's physical representation of the control room director. This person is the crew member with whom you will interact the most during a production. Remember, it is important to introduce yourself and to specify any special needs you have regarding your performance. As stated earlier, a primary responsibility of the floor director is to relay the control room director's orders with hand signals. Visual commands are an essential part of all productions because of the need to keep the environment as quiet as possible. When beginning a program, do not start before the floor director drops a hand toward you (see Figure 2). A false start will result in an *up cue*, which could chop the aural and visual introduction of your presentation.

One of the most important roles of the floor director is to make sure that talent are adjusted to the studio environment. When you first arrive at the studio, the floor director should greet you, explain some of the events that will be happening during the program, and generally ensure that you are comfortable. At the same time, he or she should check your appearance. This check often includes the observation that makeup might be needed. If you are seated, the floor directors should make sure that good posture is maintained and that clothing is smooth, not gaping or twisted. In addition, the floor director might ask that shiny necklaces, watches or pins be removed to avoid visual flares or reflection.

Microphone Dressing and Audio Checks

Whether you are a host of the show or a guest, the floor director will properly attach the lavalier microphone to you by placing the head of the microphone about six inches below mouth level. This location is a good starting point, but the lavalier could be

Figure 2
Studio Cues

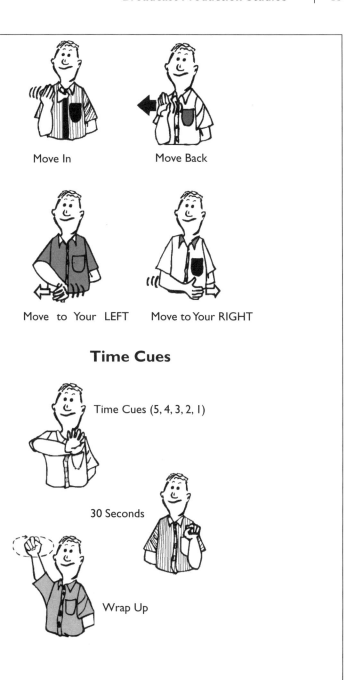

Move In

Move Back

Move to Your LEFT

Move to Your RIGHT

Time Cues

Time Cues (5, 4, 3, 2, 1)

30 Seconds

Wrap Up

Reprinted and adapted with permission of Kent State University's Teleproductions, *Television Production Assistant's Manual*, Thomas Olson, Ph.D., 1986

moved either up or down depending on the loudness of your voice. After the location is satisfactory to the audio operator, the floor director will either dress (hide) the microphone cable or explain to you how properly to do it. Generally, a small loop is made at the connector clip, and the extra cable is hidden under clothes and dropped behind you to the floor. If you are in a standing position, a small amount of gaffer tape (duct tape) is used to secure the cable to the back of your clothes and onto the floor. Proper dressing of the microphone is critical because cables can rub against your clothes and cause a rustling sound. And, obviously, cables should also be hidden for aesthetic reasons. Jewelry also creates potential for distracting noises. The solution here is to eliminate ornamental jewelry or to place microphones and cable several inches away from it.

Once the microphones have been connected, you need to do a voice level check. One common error at this stage results from voice levels deemed too soft or too loud. Unfortunately, an ill-trained floor director will ask the talent to speak more loudly or to move closer to the microphone. Talent, however, often find themselves returning to a normal voice or to a comfortable position during a broadcast. A savvy floor director and audio engineer will move the microphone closer to you rather than have you move closer to the microphone or speak more loudly. A natural environment must be created by the production staff to ensure a relaxed and professional broadcast delivery.

When microphone checks are requested by the audio operator or the floor director, try to talk at the same rate and in the same manner that you will during the performance. The old rock concert *"check, check one, check"* is used only to see if the microphone is functioning properly: *It should not test the level of your voice*! The level of your voice is best obtained if you speak in sentence form. The audio operator and the floor director will get you to talk this way by asking questions that require relatively long answers. By responding to *open-ended* requests, such as, *"Please tell me what you had for lunch today,"* or *"Please begin the first paragraph of your script,"* you become more comfortable with the studio setting, and you give the audio engineer a close approximation of your natural voice levels.

Production Assistants

In television productions, various people perform specific roles, but some crew members take on the task of helping audio engineers, camera operators, producers and lighting directors. These generalists are called production assistants (PAs), and their purpose is to function as support staff. You will find they can be very helpful to you. Most PAs are relative novices in the production environment, as many tend to be either recent college graduates or production interns. Regardless of their status, PAs provide a valuable service to both the creative/technical staff and the talent.

As talent, you will often encounter PAs in both studio and remote environments. Perhaps they will handle the cue cards you will read for a 30-second commercial or stand in for you when the lighting director needs to focus the lights on your position. Most of the time, they will handle the camera and microphone cables, carry your props and supply you with water or help in other requests. Get to know and appreciate the PAs and ask for their help.

Practice
If you have an opportunity to visit a studio or any taping location, you may want to work with the microphone to make sure you are holding it correctly or to see how a lavalier cable can be effectively hidden beneath your clothing.

Tip
Always talk with your floor director before a show. Cues vary with different people. Make sure you understand his or her cues before beginning a show.

Key Points

- Remember to get acquainted with the various microphones used in the broadcasting studio and in the field.
- Have a good understanding of the various technical jobs in broadcasting. If you know who you are dealing with, chances are your questions or comments can be dealt with in a more timely manner.

- It is essential to familiarize yourself with cues. Practice with someone so you can recognize different commands.
- Work with a TelePrompTer as much as time allows. You may not have the luxury of working with the equipment on a regular basis, so practice with the prompter operator, allowing him or her to follow your pace.
- Treat production people with respect. There is no room for talent with big egos in the broadcasting business. Always say "thank you" and respect their professionalism.

NEWS ANCHORS AND REPORTERS

In the early days of television, news reporters and anchors were not perceived to be glamorous the way they are today. In some respects, you could say that our society has placed more emphasis on TV broadcasters who are aesthetically pleasing to the viewing audience rather than on news content. Some recent studies even indicate a trend among newscasters to abandon good vocal practices, concentrating solely on appearance.[1] Perhaps this is a result of society's saturation with visual images from the media. When Edward R. Murrow was broadcasting, not every American household had a television set. The nation had no basis for comparison regarding looks. But the audience did have a comparative ratio for voice because nearly everyone had a radio; therefore, a good, strong voice was an indication of how talent rated. This chapter will tie together all the elements, including voice and appearance, that are important for news anchors and reporters. But voice and appearance must also be tied to good ethics and writing skills for a broadcaster to be successful.

On-Air Positions

It is important to know the difference between the news anchor and the reporter. The majority of recent college graduates aspire to be anchors instead of reporters. This attitude stems partially from the perception that anchors usually make more money and receive more publicity than reporters. However, aside from some exceptions, students rarely land anchor jobs right out of college. Most students will work for years as reporters before ever getting to the anchor desk.

Former news director and chairman of the Radio-Television News Director's Association (RTNDA) Gary Hanson agrees that "aspiring broadcasters need to have a realistic understanding of the business before they start marketing themselves. Otherwise, talent may set themselves up for more rejection if they have no focus."

The Reporter

If you want to be a reporter, you must have a realistic view of what lies ahead. It is easy to be overwhelmed by the pressure to make your deadline while constantly driving to different locations to get stories and trying to look camera-ready, relaxed and sound conversational. You really are a producer because you are the person responsible for calling the shots later in the editing booth and putting the package together. You must ask yourself if this "on-the-go" job is for you. Clearly, the best way to determine the rigor involved with this job is to give it a try. Experience will be the best test.

Preparation

Reporters need to know that it is important to take time to prepare their wardrobes. Weather will be a large factor in wardrobe choices. The key is to be practical, especially in rainy weather and snowstorms. You may have technical delays that force you to endure the weather extremes a little longer than you would like. What if it is 20 degrees below zero or a sweltering 100 degrees? You must appear as if you can tolerate that environment while still managing to look professional.

The solution to this quandary is to plan, plan, plan. Make sure you are equipped for every possible situation. Then, once you have your "gear" lined up, you may want to invest in back-up outfits to ensure a good look. If you happen to be on location in the middle of a hurricane, you will feel somewhat more confident if you are prepared with extra clothing. How you look is not something you want to worry about in a dangerous situation. One reporter told us that she felt the most important item to have is waterproof boots. She said there is nothing more horrible than to have to walk all day with wet feet. Sturdy boots also protect your feet at disaster scenes where there might be sharp objects, mud, or oil. Some women prefer earmuffs in the winter instead of hoods, hats or scarves because the earmuffs allow the viewers to see more of their face.

The same principle holds true for hair and makeup. If you are a reporter, you have to be more practical with your look and have a "station" where you can touch up. A station is a place in a TV van or a car where you can store a tackle box of makeup or your makeup kit, which should include a large mirror and hair supplies. Above and beyond that, you have to develop a sense of comfort in confined areas that often have poor lighting. If you have done enough air checks, you should have some indication about how much makeup you will need outdoors.

A piece of equipment you need to become very comfortable with is the **IFB**, an acronym which means **interruptible feedback**. This device is a small earpiece that reporters and anchors wear so directors can communicate with them from the TV control room during a live production. Reporters must be accustomed to walking, talking and listening at the same time. This practice takes immense concentration, but proficiency is attainable.*

---

* For more information on what you will need to pack if you are a reporter, see *Broadcast Voice Handbook* by Dr. Ann S. Utterback

Live Shots

Most of what we have discussed so far applies to live shots. Stand-ups can be pre-taped or done live, but the pressure is even more intense in the live situation. A former Cleveland news director once said that the true test of good reporters is whether they can perform good live shots.

Utterback found in a recent study that news directors are looking for people to be informative in live shots, but also conversational and spontaneous (see *Broadcast Voice Handbook*, Chapter 7, "Going Live").

Virgil Dominic, former station manager of a CBS affiliate, said preparation in live shots is paramount. "Know as much about the situation and your whereabouts as possible. Concentrate on telling the story simply—one fact leading to another so you accomplish communication with the viewer."[2] Some live stand-ups will conclude when the reporter is finished, but often, stations like a question-and-answer session to take place between the reporter on location and the anchors back at the news station. This spontaneous conversational skill can be honed by gaining talk-show experience and, of course, repetition of live stand-ups in the field.

Talking Points

Written talking points are crucial for live shots because you will be gathering information on the scene, and you must be accurate. As we will explore later in chapter five, you should use notes only as a guide to keep your facts accurate. Never read something verbatim unless you have a direct quote. You should maintain eye contact with the camera. You probably will become comfortable with a standard open and close, too. For example, you may acknowledge the anchors with an open such as: "Bob and Wendy, I'm here at 12 Street . . ." A close might be: "Reporting live from 12 Street, I'm Jim Smiles—back to you, Bob and Wendy."

Movement and Reporters

Movement is another factor to think about when you are doing a live shot or a taped stand-up for a package. Ask your videographer about the shot composition. In other words, is there enough room in the shot for you to move around? Utterback's rule for movement is *to move only for meaning and to enhance the understanding of the story for the viewer*.

Take a look at your body language. Ask yourself if you feel tense or relaxed. One of the most important things to remember is that you must be camera-ready and hold your position once you are told it is 10 seconds before you go live. Once you are in position, imagine that you are already on air. Even when your report is over, look like you are on camera until you have been told you are clear. Otherwise, you will look very unprofessional and ill-prepared. Also, always consider that the microphone is on from your stand-by cue to your close cue.

Writing

This book is not intended to teach writing skills, but it is important to mention that nothing replaces good broadcast writing. You have to make your copy sound conversational. Newspaper journalists sometimes have a difficult time making this transition if they are called to write a video script because they write for the eye, not the ear. Write what feels and sounds natural to you for conversation.

The Anchor

When it comes to wardrobe, hair and makeup, the same general principles apply for anchors, minus the outdoor gear. Reporters may look more casual than anchors do, however; as an anchor, you must be aware of the color of the backdrop for your set so your clothes contrast. Lavalier microphones are the norm for the studio anchor. And, obviously, you will be dealing with studio lights as opposed to natural sunlight, so you will have to adjust your makeup.

Movement and Anchors

While you may think it should be comfortable sitting at the anchor desk, sometimes just the opposite is true. Some talent do not know how to position their hands, while others will develop a habit of tapping the desk, playing with a pen, or shuffling papers. Often, this is not conscious movement. In fact, most talent do not even realize they have these bad habits. Air checks (viewing a tape of your performance) can be very helpful in these situations. Air check yourself regularly. Once you see what you are doing, you can try to stop. Ask a news director for additional feedback.

TelePrompTers

Utterback stresses that the anchor should be very professional but sound conversational. If you have prepared your script accordingly and have run through it a few times on the Tele-PrompTer, you should do well. The TelePrompTer is something fairly easy to master, but most first-time users forget that they, and not the operator, are setting the pace of the read (see Chapter 2). Remember, the TelePrompTer operator should always follow *your* pace!

Unfortunately, TelePrompTers sometimes malfunction and the anchor has to resort to reading off the hard copy. It is a good idea to turn the pages of your hard copy just in case technical difficulties with the TelePrompTer arise. If you are reading from the script, *always* have eye contact with the camera on the first sentence, a sentence in the middle of the copy and, most importantly, the last sentence of the copy.

Stance

Just like reporters, anchors should hold their stance (position) until their tally light goes off. If there is a miscue and you are still on camera when you should not be, the best thing to do is to glance at your news copy. Many anchors slow down the pace during the last sentence of the copy. This approach helps them bring closure to their story and cues the director that the story is finished.

Spontaneity

As with any situation in life, things do not always go as planned in television. The anchor has to be prepared for unforeseen events. Even though an anchor is simply sitting or standing at the news desk, that anchor must be aware of what is going on around him or her. For example, anchors must maintain close eye contact with the floor director and the studio monitors. Also, they should keep an eye on the studio clock. Last-minute changes take place almost every day, sometimes adding or deleting stories from the newscast. At the same time, anchors also must be delivering the news to the viewing audience in a relaxed, conversational manner! Good anchors should be able to react swiftly to these changes without showing signs of stress.

One anchor told us that a plane crash had occurred on her first day working at a large-market station. She was totally unprepared for breaking news and had a difficult time listening to directions from the control room on her IFB while simultaneously trying to read a story to the viewing audience. While she had experience with an IFB, she said sitting at the desk with all the visual distractions made it more difficult than when she was reporting in the field.

Some students seem to have a difficult time responding to changes during a broadcast. The more relaxed you are, and the more times you have dealt with these changes, the easier it becomes. Maintain a good relationship with your floor director and with your director in the control room. If hand cues are unclear, discuss the problem immediately. Repetition, however, is the prescription for an anchor who is not comfortable with spontaneity. It is like playing sports—your proficiency improves with practice.

Practice

A good way to hone your "juggling" skills as a reporter and anchor is to go to different locations and practice walking, talking and listening at the same time. Bring along a radio tuned into a talk-format station. Put an earpiece in your ear so you can hear the radio. Now, report on a story as if you were covering it live. This exercise will help to improve your concentration when you have to wear an IFB. Anchors can do the same, but they should sit at a desk.

Tip

Always have a glass of water, a powder compact and some tissue underneath your anchor desk in case of the sniffles, dry mouth, etc. Also, keep orange juice within a production assistant's reach—a full glass of cold orange juice sometimes will stop hiccups immediately.

Key Points

- Wardrobe, makeup and hair requirements are consistent between reporting and anchoring. The only difference would be with outerwear for the reporter. Follow the guidelines in this book.
- Microphone know-how is a must for the re-

porter and the anchor. Become familiar with handling the microphones.

- Live shots demand talking, walking and listening all at the same time. Get comfortable with this situation so you do not look ill-prepared.
- Talking points are important to the reporter, but do not read verbatim. Be prepared, but look relaxed and conversational. Make sure you are camera-ready before the story begins.
- Movement has to be limited in field reporting. Understand your shot composition and work with your videographer. Move only for meaning.
- Good writing skills are a must in broadcast news, but make sure you strive to write in a conversational way. You must reach the audience as what Utterback calls a "comfortable communicator."
- See that you are comfortable at the anchor desk. Are you making any unnecessary movements that may distract your viewers? Always watch your tapes.
- TelePrompTers tend to fail now and then. Be prepared to read from your copy while maintaining eye contact. Practice this often.
- Your camera stance must remain until you are clear or you see your tally light go off. Sometimes, it is helpful to slow down your pace during the last sentence of your read. This move will cue the director.

TALK SHOWS: APPEARING AS THE HOST

Many people find talk shows intriguing because they are interactive and full of surprises, especially if you have call-in questions from the viewing audience.

A Cleveland TV spokesperson recalled being asked to host her first talk show, a program about chiropractic care called "Back Talk." She was rather resistant to taking the job because she knew little about chiropractice—she had only been to a chiropractor once. The production manager was not concerned about her situation. He told her, "Visiting a chiropractor once makes you an expert—host the show." There are times when being inquisitive is the only requirement for being a good host; however, in most cases it does not replace the need for good research.

Topics

The first step in hosting a talk show is to decide on a topic. Even if you have a topic you are vaguely familiar with, you have to ask yourself what dimension of that topic will be your focus. It is like choosing a topic for a research paper or an article—it must be neither too narrow nor too broad in scope.

Your next step is to research the topic as thoroughly as possible. Do research at the library or on the Internet, and gather as many books, newspaper clippings and magazine articles on the topic as possible. Look for free brochures or pamphlets you can take advantage of by visiting different places that may provide this information. For example, if you were hosting a show on nutrition, a visit to your local health and nutrition store might be helpful. You should be able to teach yourself any given subject, because even if a producer decides on the topic, you have to take the initiative to educate yourself.

Finding Guests

Sometimes guests are scheduled through a booking producer. On the other hand, you may be saddled with finding interesting people for your show. The first criterion is to find guests who are comfortable talking in front of the camera. As with the scared professor mentioned in the first chapter, first-time guests tend to be frightened because they do not know what to expect when they appear on television. In the next chapter we will discuss how to help guests become more comfortable by educating them about being on a talk show.

Some people, however, are extremely passive or shy and do not like to talk. One way to discern whether you have a talkative guest is to call him or her on the phone. If you cannot get the person to expand on some of your preliminary questions, chances are they will not respond to you on air. Clearly, the pendulum can swing the other way—you will get someone who talks too much, but it is easier to politely cut a person off in conversation than to "squeeze blood out of a turnip."

If you have booking producers, they will handle screening prospective guests, but it also is wise for a host to talk briefly with every guest to build rapport. Author William Hagerman suggests some of the following resources, experts in specific subjects, for interviewees.[1] We have added some others to aid you in your search for guests:

POTENTIAL GUESTS

Authors	Public Relations Practitioners
Scholars	Journalists
Celebrities/Performers	Physicians
Politicians	Lawyers
CEOs	Executives/Administrators
Presidents of organizations	Experts in the field (An example would be a chef if you were doing a show about meal planning.)

If you are producing and hosting a show, when you talk with the guest prior to the show, it is imperative to give clear, accurate directions about where to come. Repeat these closer to the date in a reminder call. One host once had a guest get lost, and she had to host a show on pets by herself until he arrived. Since he was a veterinarian, she could not discuss medical issues because she was not the expert. For this reason alone, it is important to know as much about a subject as you possibly can, without, of course, pretending to be a licensed expert.

Fact Gathering

Once your guest is booked for your show, you need to find out as much about the person as possible, especially if the show topic revolves around the guest. For example, you may have a politician on your show to discuss current election issues. Maybe that individual wrote a book several years ago on a different subject that you find intriguing. While it seems people do not mind telling you about themselves, they usually do not share everything. So, you need to become a detective in fact gathering.

What resources should aid you in discovery?

1. Ask your guest for a resume or "bio."
2. Check out the Internet or your local library for old newspapers or magazine articles that include your interviewee.
3. Consult colleagues who might work with or have previously worked with your guest.
4. Request brochures or any literature your guests may have that profiles their expertise or the service they provide—read up on the subject.
5. Develop an outline to set up a question guide.
6. Call on family members or friends of your guest to aid your search. Note: Make sure your guest is comfortable with your inquiry when it comes to family, and friends. Otherwise, you might as well be an investigative reporter or a private eye!

Question Guides

Once you have assembled your data, it is time to put together a question guide for your reference. A question guide works like an outline. Many amateurs rely too much on their written questions, which lends the interview an unnatural, staged look. We suggest having an outline comprised of key words only.[2] The result of this approach is that the interview becomes more spontaneous and natural, allowing for more serendipity. One thought to remember, however, is to have more than enough key points written down just in case you discover that you are running out of issues to discuss. If your guest responds well, you probably will not need to probe those additional points or questions. Here are some points to remember when planning your guide, followed by a list of appropriate and inappropriate issues to address:

OUTLINE

I. Open
A. Introduction of show and guest
B. Thank guest for appearing

II. Middle
    A. Background information
    B. Bulk of interview (questions/
        demonstration)

III. Close
    A. Wrap-up question
    B. Thank guest
    C. Preview next show or sign off

Structuring Questions

1. Avoid closed-ended questions that might result in a yes/no answer.
Example: Do you like being a teacher?
Revised: What do you enjoy most about teaching?
Notice that the revised question allows the guest to expand on the subject.
2. Avoid sensitive questions.
Example: Did your divorce go smoothly?
Revised: Aside from some personal challenges, how have you been doing?
If you sense that in the interview you may tread on sensitive areas with your interviewee,

it is advisable to discuss the issues before the show begins. This way, you will know if the interviewee will discuss those areas or not.

3. Include questions that start off with, "Tell me . . ." Hagerman notes that this sentence lead-in has been used quite frequently by Barbara Walters.[3] This approach allows you to probe the guest for more information, but be careful not to overuse lead-in words. Vary them. Another lead-in would be, "What about . . .."

4. Avoid multiple questions.

   Example: Now, you have said that you enjoy teaching, but what about grading papers—do all the students get their projects in on time? (Basically, this asks two things: First, how do you handle grading papers? Second, do the students get their work done on time?)

   Revised: You have said that you enjoy teaching, but how do you handle grading all those papers?

   Follow-up question would be, "How do you motivate the students to hand in their work on time?"

5. Allow for follow-up or probing questions.

   Many experts encourage interviewers to follow up on interesting comments that interviewees make. Sometimes, issues surface in the interview that you do not anticipate. They come out of nowhere. A good interviewer will take these unexpected comments and probe the issue with additional questions.

6. Avoid "filler words." The most common sign of an amateur is when the host says "um" or "okay" between questions or when the interviewee pauses. Many times, hosts are not even aware they are using filler words, but their audience is! They reveal the host's nervousness. Remember, what feels like an eternity of dead

air to you is not more than seconds, which are fleeting to the viewing audience.

Broadcast instructors often have their students watch their air checks until they realize how many times they have said "um" or "okay." They can then learn to pause instead. A good way to pause is to simply look down at your question guide and look up at your guest as if you are pondering the next question. This practice is much more acceptable than using filler words.

7. Close with wrap-up question.

Hagerman refers to the wrap-up question as the "catch-all question."[4] McCoy prefers the term "wrap-up" because this type of question is very effective toward the end of a program. When the floor director gives you the one-minute cue, it is a good time to inform your guests that you have about a minute left, allowing them to answer one, final question.

Always remember that you are the one in control, not the guest. Here is a sample of an inappropriate question and a revised question for the close of the interview:

Example: Tell us about your five-year experience with the company.

Revised: We have about a minute left. Would you briefly share with the viewers your most memorable experience during your five years with the company?

8. Control a guest who talks too much.

Many people believe that it is easier to deal with this type of guest than to work with someone who is not talkative. You should explain to your guests during the warm-up that they should not feel offended if you cut them off because of commercial breaks or for any other reason. It is a good idea to mention how much time is left on the show so the guest knows not to be too long-winded. If you cannot get your guests to stop talking, it is acceptable to politely, yet with assertiveness, interrupt them. You have no other choice in this matter unless your director is kind enough to provide you with a safety window by cutting into the credits at the end of a show.

9. Make sure you check your bias.

We all have inherent biases about subjects because we have been exposed in some way to the issues, and we form opinions. Objectivity is not always easy for journalists to achieve. According to research expert Michael Patton, a good way to check your bias is to be aware that you have one.[5] When people understand they have a bias, even a slight one, they find it is much easier to keep objectivity in mind when phrasing questions. Surely, if you feel too strongly about an issue, and think you cannot avoid editorializing, it is advisable to relinquish the interview to someone else.

Settings

The setting in the studio can affect your interview style. For example, if you are doing a show where you and your guest are seated on a couch, you may find the environment promotes a sense of comfort and casualness in your interview style. On the other hand, you may be seated at a news desk to create more authority. The concept of the show dictates your style and, usually, the environment.

Another factor to consider is the camera set-up. You should know which camera you will be on at different times during the show. A good floor director will work at making you and your guest aware of the studio elements, but sometimes you may be interviewing someone on location, and there is no floor director. It is a good idea to help your camera person by making sure your guest is comfortable. Use your warm-up period with the guest for this.

Warm-Ups

A good practice before you start your show is to make your guests comfortable, especially those people who are on a talk show for the first time. While it is good to focus on the show, sometimes it is better to create "small talk." More often than not, this type of conversation reduces some of the stress that your guests may feel.

A great compliment is when your guests tell you that they were comfortable on your show because you made them feel they were going out with a friend for coffee. However, some talent in the business prefer to have their guests focus on the show. Try different approaches to see what brings you the most success.

Call-In Shows

A good example of a call-in talk show host is CNN's Larry King. In many ways, the addition of the viewer into his discussion is exciting, but this format also has its share of potential disasters because of the absence of time-delay systems which allow calls to be screened. Some stations do not have a time-delay screening system. Instead, they have production assistants screening most of the calls. If you have people who are screening the calls, a prank call might slip through to the set.

A proven strategy when getting a prank call is to react

as if nothing happened and move on to the next call. While it is difficult to act composed, viewers appreciate the professionalism. The first few times that prank or abusive calls come through will be very nerve-wracking in terms of staying focused. Be prepared! It is very difficult to focus on what the guests are saying when someone is referring to you with expletives. In time, you will be able to regain your focus more quickly, and your tolerance should grow stronger.

One technical thing to remember is to make sure you master the phone system. Otherwise, you will have unnecessary stress when you are on air. Also, remind yourself to look at the appropriate camera when a viewer calls. Many hosts look down at the phone when a caller is talking as opposed to looking at the camera (viewing audience).

Demonstrations

Even though demonstrations like cooking or refinishing furniture are fun to host, you must be careful to understand where your cameras are. Usually with a demo show, there will be some additional cameras because the director will want to get shots of you, the demonstrator, the product, and a wide shot to show the entire process and everyone involved.

Make sure you know which cameras will be covering the different subjects, including yourself. Talent feel more comfortable when they use their peripheral vision to allow them to be aware of the shot positions. For example, if you are helping with a cooking demonstration, you will want to know if you need to tip a bowl up so the camera can get a shot of its contents. The only way a host will know about shot positions is to have a studio equipped with TV monitors to use as a reference point. Again, communication with your production crew is essential.

Practice

Host a mock five-minute show, focusing on a topic of your choice. Select your guest, and gather the appropriate information. Record your interview and critique yourself.

Tip

Rehearse your open and close as much as possible—most talent find these two aspects of the show to be the most difficult. Also, watch for opens and closes that are too scripted— look and sound as natural as possible!

Key Points

- **Topics**—Decide on a topic that it is not too broad. Once you have decided on a topic, col- lect as much information about the subject as you can.
- **Fact Gathering**—The library or the Internet probably are the best places to go for your data collection. In addition, you can talk to people who associate with your guest.
- **Finding Guests**—Consider a preliminary phone warm-up with your guest to make sure you have someone who will talk. Look for guests with credentials who can expand on your subject.
- **Question Guides**—Remember to use your guide as an outline. Never read from your guide verbatim. Also, avoid closed-ended questions as much as possible, along with filler words.

- **Setting**—Understand that your studio setting may have an impact on your interview style.
- **Guest Warm-Ups**—It is always a good idea to casually talk with your guest before the show. Also, make sure your guest is camera-ready, especially if you do not have a producer.
- **Call-In Shows**—While call-in shows can add an exciting dimension to the interview, you must be ready for prank calls and have a good understanding of the phone system. Remember to look at the camera when you are talking to a caller.
- **Demonstrations**—Probably the most important thing to consider is the shot sheet for your show. In other words, where will the cameras be pointing?

TALK SHOWS: APPEARING AS A GUEST

Often, executives who are representing a company, or people who are classified as experts, are asked to participate in a talk show for television or the Internet. If you happen to be called as a guest, it is recommended that you review the previous chapter to gain an understanding of the host's perspective. If you can understand how the host will structure the interview, it makes you a better, more relaxed guest. In this chapter, we have included an overview to help you prepare to be a guest on a TV talk show.

The Booking

If you are called to participate in a talk show, you have many things to think about. The first consideration should be whether you qualify to be a guest. If you are asked to address a subject you are not familiar with, you should relinquish the opportunity to someone more credible. After all, your reputation is at stake!

If you accept the engagement, you need to take the necessary steps to prepare. These basic issues should be addressed with a producer or a host:

1. What is the date of the broadcast, and what time should you arrive?
2. Can they send directions or a map?
3. What specific areas of the topic do they want you to cover?
4. How long is your segment?
5. Will there be a makeup artist provided?

These questions should be answered during the initial phone call. You do not want to be scrambling at the last minute. We recommend asking for a confirmation letter, especially if the engagement is more than two weeks away.

Hosts and producers frequently are asked if the guest's family can attend and watch the broadcast. Policies are different in every situation, so if you want to bring your family to the broadcast, ask a producer. Keep in mind, if your family is allowed to visit, they will be directed to a specific location to watch the broadcast or be part of a live studio audience.

Finally, for anything except a news interview, clarify whether stipends are offered or your travel expenses can be reimbursed. Small TV markets are not likely to provide stipends, but they may take care of travel expenses. It does not hurt to inquire about potential compensation. You can request to be given a taped copy of the broadcast, but make sure you ask for this video in advance because TV stations do not archive tapes for a long period of time. If you wait too long, they may have bulked (taped over) the master video.

Appearance

Reviewing the "On Camera Toolbox" in the second half of this book should put you at ease with your makeup, hair and wardrobe. Some people think they do not have to wear makeup if they are the guest on a show. McCoy worked with a doctor who insisted he did not need makeup for a talk show. Unfortunately, his stubbornness resulted in his looking extremely pale during the broadcast. Even though you may not need to invest in makeup products or clothing as a host would, you should have a basic understanding of the do's and the don'ts. Remember to ask if someone will be on hand to do your makeup. The reality is that you probably will have to rely on your own skills to prepare.

Research

Although you may be the expert on the subject you will be discussing during a broadcast, you should update your information—review your research, check the Internet or go to the library. If hosts are knowledgeable, they could throw you a curve during the interview. When a host asks you a question that you are not comfortable answering or you are not sure of the correct answer, simply explain you would have to research that a bit more to respond confidently or accurately.

In addition, hosts may ask you questions that you believe could negatively affect your character or incriminate you. If you are put in this position, respond by saying you are not comfortable discussing the matter, but you would like to comment on something else. As a guest, you should leave it to the host to conduct a show's pace and the direction of content, but there should be mutual respect. If you are not comfortable with the question, do not respond—take the initiative to change the line of questioning.

Make sure you indicate to the host if there is a subject you would like to avoid. This briefing could save everyone a lot of embarrassment. However, you should discuss what you *do* want to talk about as well. For example, you may have expertise in an area of which the host is unaware.

To feel more comfortable, you also can ask the host of the show or a producer to send you some questions in advance.

This way, you will have some idea of what to expect for the show. Another tactic is to fax the host some questions you think would be appropriate. Either way, you have a better vision of what to expect. This is helpful especially if you are making your TV debut.

You might want to let the host know if you have any visuals you think would enhance the show. If you are a veterinarian and the topic is pet dental health, for example, you may have some charts or models that would help the viewers better understand what you are explaining. Do not be offended, however, if you bring an item to the show and the production assistant tells you it will not work. An example is charts that are laminated. These displays look wonderful in an office, but reflect the studio lights, causing an annoying glare.

The Set

The settings for talk shows vary enormously in size, shape, color and location. You could find yourself in a huge, high-budget studio or in a room the size of a small kitchen with a black drape for a set backdrop. Or you may be in a room the size of a closet and hooked up with an IFB to another location. And you might find yourself in a huge conference room for an Internet teleconference. While the environments are different, the same principles of TV still apply. For this reason, it is crucial to inquire about the color of the set's backdrop. You would not want to wear black on a show where the backdrop is the same color (see Chapter 11).

Your environment is another factor that you should think about. Will you be outdoors? If you are in a studio, will you be sitting in a chair or on a couch? Will the host and the other guests be with you or will you be alone, listening through an IFB and looking at a camera instead of other people? Overall, the more you know, the less fear you will have the day of the broadcast. Always try to watch or get a tape of the show prior to your appearance. This will give you a better understanding of the host's approach and the format of the show.

Preparation

Punctuality is imperative in television. The show must go on with or without you. While some crises are impossible to avoid, preparation can prevent tardiness. For example, deciding on your wardrobe in advance can save you time and aggravation. If the host is expected to be on time, then the guest should be, too. As with any appointment, you should get explicit directions to the studio or the remote site, especially if you are not familiar with where you are going.

Carry a cell phone with you, and make sure you get a contact number to call. If you are appearing on television during the weekend, you may want to get additional phone numbers because many office switchboards are closed, and you could reach an answering service. Also, carry phone numbers of taxi services and roadside-assistance companies. One executive had a flat tire on her way to an interview show. She immediately called for roadside assistance, and made it on time for the show. Another piece of advice is to have a back-up person on call should you feel it is impossible to get to the broadcast on time because of some unforeseen event or illness —things happen!

Knowing when you should arrive is beneficial, not only to be punctual, but to give yourself a preparation period. Many hosts like to take time to chat with you before the show. You may get a makeup call. Allow at least an additional hour if a makeup artist is available. There is nothing more frustrating for a makeup artist than a guest arriving too close to show time. If you look good, you will feel more confident during a broadcast. Allow ample time for makeup, wardrobe or additional instructions.

Show Time

Assuming that all goes well with your trip to the station or the remote location, you can expect to be ushered into a waiting area or a "green room"(an old theatre term). You probably will have a chance to chat with a producer and the host of the show. This pre-show period is called the **warm-up**. During this brief time you will have an opportunity to get acquainted with the host and have a bit of casual conversation. Sometimes, you may not have this moment because the staff is occupied with other last-minute details. If you did your homework, you should not worry. In fact, some people prefer not to engage in conversation right before they go on air because it makes them lose their focus and possibly become nervous (see Chapter 4). If you think you will have a case of the jitters, refer to Utterback's *Broadcaster's Survival Guide*. You will find great tips for stress reduction.

Once you are on the set, you will be attended to by a floor director or a production assistant. They will want to make sure you are at ease, and that your microphone is properly attached (see Chapter 2). Always make sure your microphone cord is tucked under your lapel or your tie. If you find yourself with a mic cord dangling from your clothing, please alert an assistant before you go on air. Once the microphone is in place, avoid getting your hands too close to it because it will produce a static sound when you are on air. In addition, if you have a cold, do not be afraid to have a box of tissue near by and a glass of water. You do not want to have additional worries when you are interviewed.

It is important for you to know where you should look during the show. If there is a host, you will generally look right at the host throughout the program. Forget that there are any cameras present and engage in comfortable conversation. If there are multiple guests, you may look at other guests when they are talking. Again, ignore the cameras. Generally, you will not talk directly into the camera unless you have been told to do so by a staff member.

Overall, if you follow these tips, you should have an enjoyable experience. We cannot reiterate enough, however, the importance of understanding the broadcast from the host's vantage point, as explained in Chapter 4. The more educated you are about this experience, the better it will be for everyone, including you.

Tips
Avoid filler words like "um" or "okay." Even though you are not the host of the program, you will appear more professional if you do not start your sentences with filler words. Take a silent pause and then answer the question.

Practice
Try running through some questions with a colleague on video tape. If you have a camcorder handy, you can effectively critique yourself on tape, along with getting some helpful feedback.

Key Points

- Review all the particulars so that you arrive on time at the correct location. Get all the time facts, compensation and other requests straight before you arrive.
- Plan ahead with wardrobe, keeping in mind the backdrop and the set environment. This knowledge also will help with color choices and fabrics.
- Research your topic and discuss potential questions with the host or a producer so you feel comfortable.
- Prepare for the unforeseen by having a back-

up guest and a cell phone with the right contact numbers.

- Always ask an assistant for help if you find your microphone cord dangling or if something else needs attention.

Enjoy yourself!

ON-CAMERA COMMERCIALS

Commercials, sometimes referred to as spots, are a good source of supplementary income. They may require on-camera appearances or simply voice-over (audio only) work. Commercials are an effective way to diversify a spokesperson's delivery style. Many news professionals experiment with commercials because the commercial may allow them to use a very bright sound as well as a lively presentation.

With a commercial, you must never be dull. The goal of the commercial is to sell or to create awareness. Practicing TV commercials is a wonderful exercise for TV news students who are having trouble bringing energy to their news read.

Even though the voice-over and the on-camera spot are very similar in terms of delivery, the visual element of the on-camera commercial presents some real challenges for talent. The first thing you should know is how the different types of TV commercials are categorized. Authors Stan LeRoy Wilson and James Wilson have suggested some of the following categories.[1] And, author Squire Fridell has added some interesting classifications.[2] We have added some categories as well.

Testimonial—Probably the most believable commercials, testimonials are effective because they incorporate spokespeople who actually have used the product.

Character—Character spots have the "character" mark the identity of the product. Everyone knows Dave from Wendy's. There are pros and cons when accepting this kind of assignment. The positive side is that you probably will have a job for a long time if you do good work. Conversely, you could get "typecast," which means that producers will have a difficult time using you for other jobs because people associate you with a product.

Plain Folks—This sort of commercial uses everyday, non-intimidating people. The reason these spots are so effective is that the consumer can relate well to these average folks rather than to a Hollywood star or an actor.

Celebrity—Whether you are a sports star, a Hollywood star, or have a connection to some famous product or service, you could be asked to endorse something on TV. Basically, you would play yourself, but you will have to try the product!

Demonstrator—This spot requires you to demonstrate the product. The client's belief is that if people see the product in use, they are more likely to be persuaded to purchase it.

Realism—This sort of commercial is like looking into someone's window or backyard as an omniscient observer. The viewer sees people in their routines, such as painting, playing football, etc. Most often, you will find multiple characters in these spots, but not always.

Character Types

As in the "industrial" (see Chapter 7), character types must be established before you pursue any kind of TV commercial work. You must be selective with your choices. Also, be true to yourself when you look into the mirror. Even though you may not be a glamorous, professional model, you may have some interesting character traits. Most agency directors find it is difficult for some people to accept that they are better suited to play a nurse or a plumber than a fashion model. If you fit a certain character type, the monetary rewards can outweigh the shock of the realization.

Think about incorporating a similar character list as suggested for the industrial in Chapter 7. This list will come in handy when we discuss marketing yourself later in this book. Here are some general character categories you can consider:

Nurse	Working Mom	Executive (male or female)
Doctor	Dad (all age ranges)	Police/Fire Personnel
Grandparent	Housewife	Teenager/Child
Secretary	Teacher	Mechanic
Ethnic/Age (Characters reflecting a certain demographic)	Fresh-Faced Youth (often used in fast-food restaurants)	

Auditions

Later in this book, you will discover some helpful tips for the audition process, however, with the on-camera commercial, it is important to mention now that you should understand your character when you get called to do an audition. One woman auditioned for a commercial for The Hoover Company, a vacuum distributor. She noticed that everyone waiting to audition looked very glamorous, and she only was dressed in jeans and a sweater, but that is what she wore when she cleaned her house. She won the audition because her vision of someone vacuuming was the most realistic. Nationally known voice and acting coach Charles Richie mentions that "When auditioning for a commercial, it is appropriate, and sometimes expected, to dress for the part. For example, you would probably wear jeans and a flannel shirt to play the role of a construction worker. Remember, the product is the star—not you!"

Preparation

It was common practice to do live commercials in the early days of television, but that approach has changed. Today it is very rare that commercials are done live or live on tape (with no stops for editing). Effects and multiple edits are now incorporated into many TV spots to hold the viewer's interest. Sometimes segments of the spot will be done out of sequence, allowing for the use of a TelePrompTer or for memorizing short segments of the copy. Usually, the director or the producer will decide what is the most practical section to start with, especially if you are on location. What if it rains? You would not want to waste an entire day trying to get shots outside if you can get some work done inside the studio.

Always go over your script until you feel comfortable with the copy. Mark words with a highlighter that you are unsure of and check for blocking directions. **Blocking** means where you will move during the commercial. On some occasions, the director will have done this work in advance, but you may get movement directions the day of the shoot.

Review the sample TV commercial script. Notice how the script is split in half, down the center with directions for video cues and audio cues (see Figure 3). Basically, one column is for text and sound, while the other is for visuals. Do not get confused with the technical notes the producer writes down—they do not concern you.

Marks and Props

One word to familiarize yourself with is **marks**. A production assistant will put pieces of tape on the floor or the demonstration table to designate where you are to stand or to place props (items on the set that you will work with). The reason marks are used is that videographers like to establish their shots in advance. The frame of the camera lens can only take in so many subjects at a time. If you move outside of your marks or put your prop down somewhere else, you and the prop could be out of the shot!

Products

Displaying products not only requires you to be aware of your marks, but also to consider what directions you receive from the floor director. You may lift up a can, for example, that reflects too much light. A director will instruct the floor director to tell you to try the move again, turning the can to the right to lessen the reflection. *If you make a mistake, do not say you are sorry*! This apology simply slows down the process and is not necessary.

Figure 3
On-Camera Commercial

ON-CAMERA :15

VIDEO	AUDIO
Storefront Shot (Talent walking)	At Walls, you can buy today and hang tomorrow.
Talent Showing Samples	We have a wide variety of styles and colors!
Interior Shot with Display Signs	V/O: Buy a double roll for the price of a single roll.
Talent in Front of Store	When it comes to buying wallpaper, it's Walls— the leader in design.
Tag/Graphic	
	FADE IN MUSIC

Reprinted and modified with Permission of Entertech Productions

The director will do as many as necessary until the winning shot is captured. A 30-second TV spot could take one to three days to shoot, depending on the requirements.

Typical Shooting Day

There is really no typical shooting day with a commercial. You could be called in for one hour or asked to be available the entire day. Make sure you bring some reading material if you are not content simply to watch how the day unfolds. Most production crews need time for food breaks, but it is a good idea to pack some fruit or a non-perishable sandwich and some water. Follow the same wardrobe and accessory suggestions provided in Chapter 7.

Voice-Overs

If you have the vocal qualities producers and advertising agencies seek, you may find yourself doing more voice-overs than on-camera work, in which you read the commercial copy while the producers add the visual elements to complete the commercial.

The challenge with the voice-over is the character you are portraying. Even a generic spokesperson must sound convincing. Some professionals believe voice-over work requires more character analysis and acting skill than on-camera work because you do not have any props or visual feedback from a studio crew. You must persuade the listeners through your voice alone, creating the product image in their minds so they are motivated to purchase whatever you are trying to sell. This is quite a task when you are sitting in a sound booth by yourself, reading copy. Utterback's "PREP" approach addresses this challenge for reporters when they prepare voice-overs for their news packages (see *Broadcast Voice Handbook*, Chapter 6). The same approach is helpful to the commercial spokesperson.

Susan Blu and Molly Ann Mullin, experts and authors on voice-over training, developed a formula called *The Basic Process*.[3] They encourage broadcasters to do the following:

- Focus on energy.
- Visualize the copy.
- Decide what character is speaking.
- Discern what is happening in the spot.
- Note at which point the sales pitch is given.

- Envision the environment.
- Ask yourself why you are doing the commercial.

For more information on voice-overs, see Suggested Readings.

Timing

Most commercials run at 15 seconds, 30 seconds or 60 seconds. A stopwatch is a must for anyone interested in voice-over work. You must learn to time yourself. Many production houses and radio stations are switching to computerized audio systems (digital), allowing talent to keep track of time without the use of a stopwatch; however, stopwatches are good to have on hand for practice.

A good rule to follow is to "clock out," or finish your read, two seconds before your time is up. For example, if you are reading a 30-second commercial, you should finish the copy at 28 seconds. This two-second window allows the producers to insert music or graphics if it is a television spot.

Radio and TV stations are very concerned with exact timing because they are allowed a specific block of time to air the commercials. The most common mistake for beginners is to run over the allotted time. The spots must be accurately timed so the station can go into a program at the appropriate time. Many professionals tell us they can actually feel when it is 28 seconds or 58 seconds when cutting a voice-over. This instinct comes from experience.

Repetition is the key to honing your skills. McCoy tells many of her students to volunteer for voice-over work at local radio stations. Reading spots that are high energy, hard sells, or public service announcements (PSAs) about something serious like cancer awareness, you will have the opportunity to experience different types of commercial copy. The more flexible you are with your reading style, the more you will be employed as a voice-over artist.

Donuts

The **donut spot** is probably the most challenging commercial to read. When you receive your copy, you will notice that the first section has seconds allocated for your read. Then, there is a section in the middle of the spot that allows for music (a hole). Toward the end of the commercial, you will see more copy for you to read (see Figure 4).

Sometimes, the copy looks just the opposite. For example, the commercial may begin with music, allowing some time in the middle of the copy for you to speak, and close the spot with more music. Either way, this spot can be very tricky because you have to clock out on time or your voice will run over the music or the jingle. A **jingle** is where singers are brought in to sing a theme song for the advertiser. Jingles are very lucrative for broadcasters, but you have to be able to sight read music and have extensive vocal training in order to land those jobs.

> *Practice*
> Create a 15-second script to work with, and go through all the elements of the TV- commercial process. Practice working at a table with a bottle of dish detergent, a dish towel and a dish. You should have blocking movements with marks on your table. Try to work with a camcorder so you can record yourself. The goal is to maintain eye contact with the camera, stay with your marks, create fluid movements when you work with the product, and persuade your viewers to purchase the product because of your convincing presentation.

Figure 4
Donut Spot

RYAN'S: 30 SPOT

VIDEO	AUDIO
RYAN'S GRAPHIC	MUSIC (5 sec.)
GENERAL SHOTS OF BAR	RYAN'S . . . YOUR NEIGHBORHOOD BAR AND GRILL WHERE YOU CAN RELAX
GRAPHIC	ENJOY DANCING TO BLUES OR CLASSIC ROCK EVERY NIGHT
PEOPLE DANCING	DON'T FORGET, TUESDAY IS LADIES' NIGHT AND OUR WEEKLY DANCE CONTEST!
SHOTS OF PEOPLE EATING	FOR GOOD FOOD AND GREAT ENTERTAINMENT, RYAN'S—IN SILVERTON
GRAPHIC	MUSIC (5 SEC.)

Reprinted and modified with permission of Entertech Productions

Tip

Always remember to hold your "stance" (position) at the end of the commercial until the director says "cut." So, if you are smiling and holding a product, you have to remain in that stance until you are cleared. Also, you must be "camera-ready" (in position to start taping) before the director cues you to start. You should assume this position when you get a starting count-down from the floor director.

Key Points

- Understand the different types of commercials. Which type of commercial are you doing?
- Assess your character types. Would you be comfortable portraying these roles?
- Make sure you dress the part of your character when you audition.
- Prepare appropriately for your shooting day. Make sure you are comfortable with the copy.
- Get clear directions regarding your marks and blocking.
- Practice working with props if you have time. Make sure to stay within your marks.
- Take care of yourself the day of a shoot because you can get very tired.

INDUSTRIAL VIDEOS

Many people in video use the term *industrial* rather freely, but not everyone really understands what practitioners are talking about. It is important to clearly define the meaning of industrial before explaining how talent participate in the process. The term refers to corporate video, non-commercial video or business video. Basically, an industrial means video intended for business use, usually used "in-house." Some industrials are used for training employees, for example. One would not find this type of video on the major commercial TV networks, CNN or PBS. Often, corporations will use industrial videos in place of internal newsletters, serving as a form of corporate communication. Some larger companies actually have an in-house video production facility, while other businesses subcontract the work to independent video production houses. In this type of video, the company PR practitioner or the CEO sometimes appears on camera. Video topics can range from providing safety training tips to improving customer relations. "Point of purchase" videos, considered industrials, are also very popular to use in exhibits at trade shows or in retail.

As mentioned earlier in this book, industrials did not infiltrate the corporate world until the 1970s, when video equipment became more portable.[1] Now, the use of videos in the business world has become pervasive. In the first chapter, you discovered that new technologies have provided even more opportunities for people to appear on video. Keep in mind that videos are not just one component of a multimedia program or an Internet segment, but an aspect of the process that is vital to maintain that "people connection," something that straightforward computer graphics cannot do.

The Product

One challenge in working as talent in an industrial is that you have to understand and be able to pronounce the jargon. You may get called to do a shoot for a company that produces *digital video* and *auto interfaces*—what is that? Whether you work for the company or not, you must have a grasp of the product and the correct pronunciations of the technical terms. Many times, a producer will make sure your pronunciation is accurate, but it is a good idea, if time allows, to review your script to see if there are any words or concepts you question. Write the correct pronunciations phonetically on your copy.

One talk show host was called to do a video for a computer company when personal computers were in their infancy. This was a very challenging opportunity because not many companies had personal computers in their offices. Terms that commonly are used today in the office regarding a computer, such as "gigabytes," were total jargon. A producer had to be on location all the time to check for inaccuracies in pronunciation.

In light of the pronunciation issues, many companies prefer to use someone internally to appear on camera. Executives or employees who never have been on camera face the challenge of being able to effectively perform in front of the camera.

Environment

Industrials can take you to strange locations. Sometimes you will be asked to wear a hard hat if you are hosting a safety video. Wardrobe is a key issue when considering your environment. Not all footage is shot in a traditional studio setting. What if you are called to host a promotional video for a resort in the Caribbean? This type of shoot cries out to have an appropriately dressed host walking along the beach or guiding the viewer through some resort.

Walking and talking at the same time can be difficult for some people. If you are given this type of on-location assignment, it is a good idea to practice walking as you are trying to memorize the copy. Do not rely on a TelePrompTer to be available at on-location shoots. While portable field cameras and TelePrompTers are used on some shoots, they tend to be very expensive to rent or own.

Many videos are requested during "the eleventh hour." In other words, there is often very little time to write a script and get the project done. While the ideal is to have a video script in advance to ensure adequate memorization, this is not always possible.

Cue cards are an option to guide talent, but they are not producers' favorite approach because of the poor eye contact. Cue cards have to be positioned toward a side of the camera lens; therefore, the host does not directly look at the lens. The result of this practice is that the talent's eyes look as if they are shifting to the right or the left of the viewer's television screen.

Ear Assist

Another device that talent can use to prompt their scripts, especially on remote productions, is *ear assist*. According to Dale Young, owner of Hearing Instrument Services and the creator and national distributor of a *wireless* ear assist called *The PromptEar*, "This instrument primarily was used by the Federal Bureau of Investigation until the 1980s. The industrial video companies saw the benefits of this device in that it could replace the TelePrompTer, especially at remote locations where it is difficult to bring a lot of cumbersome equipment."[2]

To use an ear assist, the host must read the script into a mini tape recorder. After the tape is played back for accuracy in pronunciation and delivery pace, the tape recorder is fastened with a clip to the talents' waist. The earpiece can be custom molded for size and skin color. In addition, the earpiece is powered by special batteries and is easily inserted into the ear. When it is time to appear on camera, the talent provide a lead-in count for the producers, push the play button and recite the script on a one-second delay, while the recorded delivery of the script is playing in the spokespersons' ears!

There are some tips to remember if you attempt to incorporate this device:

- You must practice extensively! Young says, "Practice in front of a mirror. Make good eye contact, and avoid looking 'zoned out' while listening to your script." Do not say you are proficient in ear assist if you are not smooth with your delivery. This process is like practicing a musical instrument—you would not perform in a recital if you did not master the instrument.

- Make sure you have appropriate, functional equipment. There is nothing worse that having your equipment fail in the middle of a shoot. Always have an extra set of batteries just in case.

- Watch your delivery pace. On occasion, some people read copy at a different pace than when they are in front of a camera. Play back your taped read several times to make sure you are comfortable. Also, check to see if you can hear yourself, but be careful not to make it too loud because the recording will bleed into the audio used for the video. If you are working with other talent, try to be sensitive to people who are not using ear assist. You still must be able to react to them in a natural manner.

Note: While the concept of ear assist is great, many producers have reported that the finished product looks very unnatural and robotic. One easily could understand why the result is rather artificial looking because the talent may be focusing too much on just getting the words out, or their pre-recorded delivery pace may not be in sync with their live presentation pace. Also, ear assist is rarely used in news reporting or live shots. Reporters strive to look as spontaneous as possible in front of the camera. The only way to really look convincing and be effective with ear assist is to practice, practice, practice.*

Content and Delivery

The one element that sets the industrial apart from the news story is the content. Sometimes the industrial is referred to as a cross between a commercial and a news story. While you may be informing the public about the issues, you may be soft selling them, too. For example, McCoy was contracted to read an industrial for a local hospital's rehabilitation program. The goal of the video was to make the patients feel better about the recovery period that was ahead of them, but also to soft sell them on the in-house rehabilitation program.

Essentially, talent must convey the spirit of the video with their delivery. If there is not enough of a conversational sound, you may lose the viewing audience's attention (see Chapter 13).

---

* For more information about the *PromptEar*, see Suggested Readings and Information.

When coaching corporate people for industrials, Utterback stresses the need to be a comfortable communicator. This disposition enhances the credibility of spokespeople, while making them appear very human and accessible.

A sample of an industrial script is provided, along with scripts for a hard news story and one for a commercial (see Figures 5, 6 & 7.) Practice each aloud. You should notice a difference in your approach to each read. The news story should have a conversational yet serious tone, probably read at a slower pace. The commercial should render a bright, energetic sound, probably fast-paced. The industrial should fall somewhere between the two extremes. There are, however, exceptions to this rule. For example, you may be called to sit at a news desk in an industrial, as if you were an anchor. In situations like this one, you must think about your character.

Character

Like the commercial, the industrial usually calls for you to portray someone. You may find yourself playing a news anchor or a physician. There is no question that wardrobe choices can help with your character, but you must, most importantly, feel comfortable and act believably. One spokesperson was asked to be a fully-clothed demonstration model for an OB/GYN equipment video. Thankfully, the shoot was done in good taste, but it was not a job she wanted to do again. As talent, you have to ask yourself what you are comfortable doing.

Auditions

As with commercial, you should dress appropriately and be true to your character. Also, be prepared for a "cold read" when you

Figure 5
Hard News Story Sample

```
SHUTTLE WAKE-UP TAL: EM PG. 29 SEQ: 31

(DATE)                  ((    ))

A:                      THE DISCOVERY ASTRONAUTS
                        AWOKE FOR THEIR FINAL
                        DAY IN SPACE THIS
                        MORNING.
                        ((TAKE V/O NATS))

# From Discovery/9849  AFTER AN EIGHT-DAY
                        MISSION TO REPAIR THE
                        HUBBLE SPACE TELESCOPE,
                        THE ASTRONAUTS ARE
                        PREPARING TO RETURN
                        HOME.

                        THE TRIP WAS CUT SHORT
                        BY LAUNCH DELAYS . . .
                        AND ONE OF THE SPACE
                        WALKS WAS CANCELLED.

                        BUT THE ASTRONAUTS
                        STILL MANAGED TO
                        INSTALL NEARLY 70-
                        MILLION DOLLARS WORTH
                        OF EQUIPMENT.

                        NASA HAS DECLARED THE
                        MISSION A SUCCESS.
```

Figure 6
Commercial Script Sample

```
A.S.A. HEALTH SPOT-1 :30

VIDEO                    AUDIO

Pan from sign to    V/O  The A.S.A. Health
building                 Rehab Center is
                         committed to the total
                         rehabilitation process.
Secretary shot      V/O  Our team of professionals
                         is dedicated

Pool shot           V/O  to providing you with
                         maximum results through
                         the use of our therapeutic
                         treatments plus our
                         invigorating aerobic
                         pool session.

Various exercise    V/O  We also offer work
room shots, and          conditioning programs
machine shots.           to get you moving
                         fast!

Shot of couple      V/O  Call A.S.A. Health
                         today and become a
                         new you!

End Tag:

A.S.A. HEALTH Rehab Center
1-800-ASA-9999
```

Reprinted and modified with permission of Entertech Productions

Figure 7
Industrial Script Sample

THE VICTORY FORMULA
Video for Prospective Benefactors

VIDEO	AUDIO
Fast Cuts	MUSIC THEME 1
	(NETWORK 104—8)
VTR: Kids at recess VRT: Stop sign	NARRATOR: Conventional wisdom about why students do poorly in school sometimes points to things like culture and economic status.
VTR: Boy Running	With your help, Sawsen Schools can change by applying our *Victory Formula*.
VTR: Red Light VTR: Soundbite 1 VTR: Soundbite 2 VTR: Location Soundbite/NAT 33	Up with Music Fade down music, bring in 1 Bring in 2 Fade out music, bring in NAT sound/33
Narrator in front of school	NARRATOR: Let's consider our accomplishments before we look at the areas in need of improvement: First, we'll examine the success of the "Xeluei" project.

Narrator	Second, we'll look at the benefits of the Margaret Smrcina endowment.
Narrator	And, third, we'll see how the coordinator of the cultural arts program has made learning innovative and exciting for students.

Reprinted and adpated with permission of Kent State University Teleproductions

go for an audition. Sometimes you will have a couple of minutes to review your script. It is acceptable to ask a producer or a casting agent how to pronounce some very technical terms; however, if you do not have this advantage, read the copy with authority. In other words, do not hesitate and stumble over the jargon, even if you know you are not pronouncing the words correctly. Your confidence and your conviction in the read will be noticed. Pronunciation can be addressed later, if you get the job.

Clothing

Clothing can help create your character. The rule for the industrial is the same as with the commercial: Come prepared with several styles and color choices. Have an iron handy for those on-location shoots, too. Since you have to bring everything from accessories to makeup, unless you have a makeup artist and stylist on hand, it is a good idea to prepare for anything.

Teleconferences and Distance Learning

More and more CEOs, office personnel, and educators are participating in teleconferences and distance learning either on TV or the Internet. In simple terms, this is an electronic approach to conducting a meeting or teaching a class—people do not have to leave their location. Instead, the instructor or the executive can conduct sessions from a distance. However, many professionals are intimidated by the approach because they have to be on camera. Similar spokesperson principles should apply to this setting:

- First, understand where your cameras are and when you are "live." Live means that you are live on camera and people can see you. So, watch that you are not yawning when you are supposed to be on camera!
- Second, prepare your conference or lecture as you always would, but make sure you have assistance with visuals you may want to include. Usually, visuals are taken care of prior to a presentation—ask your production assistant to "call them up" when you require them. This request means that the assistant will get them from **still store** (the images are recorded on another tape or put into a computer).
- Third, it does not hurt to make a **dry run** (a practice session that is not live) of your session so you know what to expect.
- Finally, wardrobe and makeup requirements are the same as prescribed in chapters 9 & 11.

The Internet

While the Internet is, as Robert Samuelson has said, "too young for anyone to foretell its ultimate significance," it has become a part of business life worldwide.[3] As pointed out in this book, the Internet is going to offer expanded "on-air" opportunities for business purposes. What executives need to realize is that, while new technology has advantages, it also has shortcomings.

According to Dr. Gordon J. Murray, director of new media at Kent State University, what you really need to understand is how the "electronic presentation is distributed." For example, if executives want to videotape themselves and distribute it through the Internet, they should understand that the image may lose some of its luminance and overall size and quality. On the other hand, if a broadcast is distributed on CD-ROM, the finished product would be far superior. In light of these technical concerns, he recommends executives work with people who have the technical knowledge to produce a quality image.

The most important thing to consider is that *all the principles for on-air presentations apply to the Internet*, whether you are participating in a local talk show, a corporate presentation or a simple video e-mail. With the exception of environmental concerns like lighting and weather, makeup and wardrobe rules remain constant, regardless of the electronic distribution choice. There is no reason why you should *not* consider all the wonderful technologies that are available, but be aware of the various nuances that occur with the end results.

Practice

As with the commercial, make a list of six character types you could play in an industrial. Support your choices.

Tip

If you have trouble memorizing your copy, break it up into small sections. Do not move ahead until you have mastered each section. Also, try to review your script in advance, and go through the copy with a highlighter. Mark any words that you are not sure how to pronounce or that present difficulty in your read. Write them in phonetics.

Key Points

- **Product**—Understand what you are representing. Make sure you prepare by reviewing your script, earmarking any difficult words to pronounce, etc.
- **Environment**—The environment can dictate your wardrobe, and also the amount of movement required. Ask your producer about the shooting environment so you can prepare accordingly.
- **Ear Assist**—If you plan to use ear assist, the most important things to remember are to practice until you are proficient and make sure your equipment is functioning well.
- **Delivery**—Producers should give you an idea about the style of read they are trying to achieve. Consider asking the producer about delivery before you practice the copy.
- **Character**—Define what character types you are for the industrial. This will aid you in deciding whether or not to accept certain jobs.

FILM AND TV ACTING

Imagine learning lines for one scene of a TV show or a film. It seems pretty simple—learn the lines, rehearse and shoot the scene. Unfortunately, film and TV acting are much more complex. For example, if cost is not prohibitive, many scenes are shot from four to six different angles. The reason for this variety of shots is for post-production editing. Directors may want to show a close-up and then go to a wide shot. Actors must repeat the same performance until the director has the optimum shots. Think about consistency when conveying emotions. If your character cries in a scene, how do you continually repeat a convincing performance?

Technique

The most difficult thing about acting for film or TV is understanding the different acting techniques, and there are many that have surfaced in the past century. We will explain one of the most popular types of acting techniques, the *Method* approach, a system devised by Russian actor Constantin Stanislavski, co-founder of the Moscow Art Theater. The *Method* technique was adapted and popularized in America during the 1930s by an organization called *The Group Theatre*, known for its focus on realism. Edwin Wilson has outlined some of the characteristics of Stanislavski's system.[1] We have condensed and modified some of Wilson's points:

1. **Relaxation**—Performers must be relaxed, releasing any unwanted tension.
2. **Concentration**—Performers must be so concentrated and focused that they lose sense of an audience even existing.
3. **Specific Activities**—Every character has specific emotions and reactions. Do not generalize your approach.
4. **Inner Truth**—Stanislavski focused on "if" when trying to achieve characters. In other words, "If I were on trip to Europe . . ." How would a person feel in that situation?
5. **Emotional Recall**—Actors can draw from their past experiences, recapturing emotions. For example, if you were portraying a doctor in a hospital for an industrial, maybe one of your parents was a doctor when you were growing up or maybe you know a doctor. Since you lived through their experience vicariously, you could "call up" those experiences and emotions associated with that character.
6. **The Inverted Pyramid**—Journalists refer to the *inverted pyramid* writing style when composing a story. Basically, you need to know who, what, where, when, how and why in descending order of importance to write a story. Method acting is similar in that actions have to be justified. For example, *what* motivates your

character to place paper on the table? *How* do you plan to execute the action?

7. **Voice and Body**—Stanislavski endorsed strong vocal techniques, along with a sensitive body. The goal was to allow actors' bodies to react to environmental stimuli. If your character was in a steam bath, for example, how would the body react?[2]

8. **Objectives**—The needs and wants of characters lead them to pursue an objective (intention) achieved through actions (beads). This progression directs them to an overall super-objective (ultimate goal), something helpful when breaking down a script.

Some practitioners consider the *Method* approach to be somewhat confusing for people who want to go into TV commercials and industrials. McCoy's approach to acting techniques and character analysis is user-friendly, incorporating some of Stanislavski's system, along with a modified checklist devised by author Marsh Cassady.[3] The following is a worksheet, modeled after Cassady's, for anyone who has to assume a character on video or TV.

ACTOR'S PROFILE

Character's Name _____

Sex _____

Age _____

Race/Ethnicity _____

Geographic Location _____

Education _____

Socioeconomic (Job) _____

Marital Status _____

Immediate Family _____

Emotional Disposition _____

Character Traits (Accent, lisp, etc.)_____

Relationship to Others _____

Additional Comments _____

After you have profiled your character, you then can interject some of Stanislavski's points. This "profile" approach is adapted by many experts in theatre. The categories can vary, depending on the individual. Perhaps there are other elements that you would like to include. The bottom line is what works for you.

Stage vs. TV and Film

Many film directors find that the most difficult aspect of working with theatre actors is to get them to minimize their actions for TV and film. Actor and director Michael Caine describes how to accomplish this sense of "smallness" by explaining that if a director can tell you are rehearsing with someone, you are overacting. When you act, you must look and sound like you are merely conversing. Caine believes that less is better.[4] It is interesting that this natural disposition is also effective in a newscast.

The main difference between TV, film and the theatre stage is that TV and film are more intimate, and you do *not* have to overstate anything, whether it is a newscast or a soap opera. Conversely, the stage demands more boldness because you have to project to the back of the theatre. However, one operatic per-former said that a director told her when she performed the role of Rose Maurrant in the opera *Street Scene*, that she was "broadcasting" on stage. You also can overdo it on stage; how-ever, this example is probably an exception to the rule.

Another difference between the stage and video is that not all video programs are live. You have time to fix the bad takes. **Take** is a term that refers to the number of sequences shot on video. As we mentioned at the beginning of this chapter, the direc-tor decides which take is the best for the completed film or video

Many theatre students and professionals who study in television performing have a difficult time adjusting to the medium. They tend to perform an industrial or a soap opera scene as if they were preparing for one of Hamlet's soliloquies—it is too much! Nationally known soap opera, film and stage actor Mark La Mura believes that the most complex moment is when a TV director tells theatre actors that they have "this much" space instead of the stage. "You have to pull the performance into your eyes." This advice is excellent because the close-up shot is imper-ative in film and TV. Energy must come through the eyes.

Script Analysis

Once you feel comfortable with acting, you are ready to analyze your script. There are numerous ways to approach script analy-sis, but you should strive to keep it simple. Go through the entire script, if possible, to get a feel for the story or the commercial. Label what qualifies as the beginning, the middle and the end. Once you have reviewed the material, identify your speaking parts and highlight them. Take each part of the script and break it down into sections. Incorporating some of Stanislavski's sys-tem and the information from your character analysis, deter-mine your environment and the character's emotions. Finally, memorize your copy until you almost cannot bear to look at it any longer.

Sides

Film producers do not always provide actors with the entire script. If you get a portion of a script, you are receiving a side (see Figure 8). Many actors find sides very difficult to work with because the scene is out of context. In other words, they do not get a feel for the entire script. How do you fully understand your character if you do not understand the entire story?

National TV and film actor and drama coach Rohn Thomas believes that ". . . getting a film side is like being given four pieces of a 500-piece puzzle, and being asked to describe the picture." Thomas explains that you must be creative in filling the gaps.

Ask advice from your agent or the casting director. Talk to other actors who have different sides. Make your best guess, then make up the rest, but make a decision—be someone.

Another challenge with film and TV acting is the shooting schedule. Thomas adds, "Film is routinely shot out of sequence. Location is the main factor in establishing shooting schedules. If your character appears in the same apartment in two scenes that span five years, both scenes will be shot before the crew moves on. This decision is dictated by economics more than anything else. This same protocol holds true for infomercials and commercial work."

Memorization, Listening and Reacting

If you are involved in a shoot that will be produced out of sequence, it is a good idea to practice memorizing the copy out of order. Again, take each section one at a time. Do not proceed with the other lines until you have mastered each section. If you have a dialogue section with multiple characters, sometimes a tape recorder is beneficial. You simply record the other person's lines and leave some space on the tape where your line would fit. Repeating this process allows for the script to become one with you.

Figure 8

Sample Script Side

PAROLE BOARD

INT - SHAWSHANK HEARINGS ROOM - DAY (1957)

Red enters, ten years older than when we first saw him at a
parole hearing. He removes his cap and sits.

                         MAN #1
                It says here you've served thirty
                years of a life sentence.

                         MAN #2
                You feel you've been rehabilitated?

                DA

                         D.A.
                You have the right to remain
                silent. If you give up that
                right, anything you say will be
                used against you in court...

                         D.A. (O.S.)
                Samuel Norton? We have a warrant
                for your arrest! Open up!

                DUTY GUARD

Troopers hustle the hapless duty guard to Norton's door as he
fumbles nervously with a huge key ring.

                         DUTY GUARD
                I'm not sure which one it is...

From "The Shawshank Redemption" by Frank Darabont.

Used with permission.

While actors in theatre are encouraged to genuinely *listen* and *react* to one another, this practice is more demanding in film and TV. Remember, directors probably will want to shoot the same scene from many angles in order to get a wide shot, a close-up and a variety of other shots. They key is to recognize that your reactions do not have have to be "big." Sometimes, a mere piercing look with your eyes could suffice as a strong enough reacton to another actor to capture the essence of the scene.

Blocking and Movement

Blocking a scene or a commercial (designating where you will stand or move) is part of the memorization process because rehearsing your movement also can help your recall. Always write your blocking cues on your script in pencil just in case the director would like to make a change in the original blocking. Once the blocking is set, you can practice anywhere. In fact, many soap operas and Broadway shows practice in warehouses or rehearsal studios because the theatre or the TV studio is too expensive to rent. Keep in mind that you need to rehearse movement and that most directors do not like to give you blocking instructions twice.

Some performers have problems deciding where to put their hands when they are talking. If you have this difficulty, take a movement course in theatre at a local college or community theatre. A workshop like this will allow you to know how to use your body in a comfortable way. News directors even have problems with anchors on the set because they do not know where to put their hands. One suggestion is to think about the motivation for your movement. If you think there is a purpose for crossing your arms, then your movement is justified. However, if you cross your arms because you do not know what to do with them, your movement looks unnatural. The answer is to embrace as much education about the craft as possible.

Props

Props can really help to develop your character. In film, it is important to remember where you put your props and how you handled them for continuity (consistency) in the multiple takes filmed in one day. If you handle your props differently in each take, the director will have a continuity problem. Films usually have a continuity person, but no one remembers how you handled your props better than you.

One difference between film and TV is the use of the slate board, which identifies the take number. Film directors like to know what take they are on during the editing process. These days, you can find digital boards being used on a set, but some directors are more traditional and prefer to use the slate board with takes marked in chalk. Also, sometimes the lead-in cues from the crew can be different in film than in TV. You may hear "Sound, speed, roll and action!" used more often in film instead of "Stand by, in three, two, one and cue," more commonly heard in broadcast TV. Nevertheless, be prepared for anything. Understand that directors are different with their production cues no matter what medium you are involved with. Learn what the game plan is for your shoot.

Maintaining Energy

Shoots for films, infomercials and soap operas can be taxing on performers. It is not unrealistic to work 14-to-16-hour days. Actors must take care of themselves during a shooting schedule. Enjoying an evening out before a big shooting day can take its toll on the performer both physically and emotionally.

Film companies are very generous when it comes to providing food, but be careful because some of the crew's choices can be high in calories. Fruit, health bars and a lot of water are excellent choices to take with you for these grueling days. Avoid too much caffeine because you do not want to come across as jittery on camera or to dehydrate yourself. If you are lucky enough, you may even get a trailer (a mobile unit, usually like an apartment) so you can rest. Trailers are ideal, but they usually come with high-budget films, and you must be one of the major stars in the production to get access to one.

Being a TV performer is like being an athlete—you constantly have to be in training. Whether you are a reporter, a PR spokesperson for a company or a soap-opera actor, you have to be camera-ready and at your best all the time. Utterback's book, *Broadcaster's Survival Guide*, gives guidelines on keeping yourself in peak condition for broadcasting.

Understand that the opportunities for talent are abundant. McCoy tells her students that regardless of their interests, they need to appreciate each medium. Often, jobs are scarce in the TV business, but if you are versatile, you can adapt to every medium and make money. It is not uncommon to find a news anchor who has cut a few commercials, or an actor training to become a reporter. What about the executive who must act in an Internet video scene to train new employees? As new media blur together, these areas of performance also overlap, allowing many people to experience the best of all worlds!

Practice

Find a script that interests you. Take a portion (side) of that script, and try to go through the entire process we have outlined, incorporating the suggestions offered. Plan to give two types of performances: First, perform the scene as if you are in front of a large audience. Second, after you have completed the stage version, try taking the copy and performing it for TV. Make notations of what you did differently.

Tip

When you watch TV dramas, observe how well the actors *listen* to each other and *react*. Try to become a better listener and reactor, especially if you are working with another performer. If you observe enough, you should improve your own performance.

Key Points

- Work on developing an approach to acting. Practice as if you are an athlete in training.
- Consider your character when you are assigned a role. Make sure you do a thorough analysis of the character.
- Be able to determine the differences between stage acting and TV and film acting, especially if you have a theatre acting background.
- Review your scripts thoroughly and highlight them. Make sure you have your lines and your blocking committed to memory. Also, try to genuinely listen and react to other actors because a reaction shot may be selected by the director in the final edit session.
- If you are working with props, pay attention to your marks and the continuity in each take.
- Understand that shoots can be very draining on a performer. Take care of yourself, and come equipped with bag of non-perishable, healthy snacks to sustain your energy throughout the day, along with a lot of water.

ON-CAMERA TOOLBOX

- ✔ Makeup

- ✔ Hairstyles

- ✔ Wardrobe

- ✔ Broadcast Voice

- ✔ Sounding Conversational

- ✔ The Business -- Tips

ON-CAMERA MAKEUP

If you are considering work on camera, it is helpful to take an introductory course or a one-day workshop in television production. It helps to understand what takes place behind the scenes in order to be more effective in makeup application, microphone placement, etc. (see On-Camera Opportunities). While a course in theatrical stage makeup is sure to be beneficial, there is a difference between the stage and the TV studio when considering makeup.

The cardinal rule in television is to look natural, whereas the stage requires individuals to look more pronounced with makeup because the face has to reach the view of the audience in the last row of the house. A good rule for television is that if viewers make comments on makeup, the application is done incorrectly.

The other difference worth noting between the stage and the TV screen is the use of character makeup. Most people who are called to do a video for a corporation probably will not work with artificial beards or need to create an older look as they might in the theatre. Nevertheless, many people who have not been in front of the camera think it is like the stage when it comes to makeup. Perhaps this is because many people have been in a high school play or a college drama at some point in their lives. They are not exposed to other types of makeup application. For example, think of a news anchor with far too much blue eye shadow who looks as if she were getting ready to perform on a big proscenium stage. Viewers cannot focus on what she is saying because they are distracted by the appearance of her eyes.

Remember, not all stations or production companies provide makeup artists. What if a television station comes to your office? Will you be camera-ready? Men generally do not wear every-day makeup. How can people be ready with makeup when the occasion calls? It is important to form your own approach. Basically, it does not matter to any producer or news director how you apply makeup, but the finished result is important. And what is the best approach to makeup application? Use the following information and try to sample different products until you find something you like. The guide should serve as a foundation for both men and women so they can feel confident in applying basic makeup for television performance.

SUPPLIES

Small tackle box (to store makeup)	Concealer
	Base
Cotton balls (Powder puffs)	Blush
Cotton swabs	Brushes (set)
Powder	Lipstick and Liner
Witch hazel	Eye shadows
Alcohol	Eyebrow pencils
Makeup remover or cleanser	Moisturizer for face
Pencil sharpener	Moisturizer for eyes
Mascara	Pencil with rubber tip
Tissues (Baby Wipes)	for eyes

Small tackle box—This box is a handy and portable way to carry your makeup, especially in freelance work or if a television crew is coming to the office on short notice.

Cotton balls and Powder puffs—You will need cotton balls to remove any makeup you might have on or use them to set your powder. Also, powder puffs, dabbed in a little bit of powder, work well to set your concealer and your entire face. Make sure to shake off excess powder from your applicators.

Cotton swabs— Cotton swabs are great as applicators. Sometimes you may be out of the applicators that usually are provided in eye shadow compacts. Cotton swabs will serve as excellent applicators for blending and eye shadow application. Also, these applicators are more sanitary if multiple people are using the same product.

Witch hazel—Witch hazel is probably the most inexpensive astringent around. It is great right after cleansing the skin because it closes the pores, allowing fewer impurities to get into the skin.

Alcohol— Always have alcohol on hand for sanitary purposes. In addition, you can try dry, gel-like hand sanitizers like *Purell*. These sanitizers are wonderful because they are less drying to the hands than rubbing alcohol. Brushes should be washed and sprayed with alcohol regularly if you are applying makeup on someone else.

Makeup remover (cleanser)—You should always cleanse your skin prior to makeup application. Makeup application is much better on clean skin. It is like priming a wall for wallpaper or paint—the finished product always looks better when it is prepped appropriately.

Face moisturizer—The same rule applies as with makeup remover. You should have a good foundation over which to apply your base makeup. Your overall look improves when moisturizer is applied prior to base. Essentially, the look is more smooth and even.

Eye moisturizer—The eyes tell everything! Moisturizers can soften fine lines. You will notice that concealers (makeup used to cover dark circles) work better if the eyes have been prepared because there is less chance of creasing.

Facial tissue and Baby wipes—Facial tissue can be used for makeup removal or as a "table cloth" to put your makeup on to keep your makeup area clean. Baby wipes, non-scented and alcohol free, also are great to have on hand because they require no water or make-up remover.

Concealer—Exactly as the word is defined, this cream base is used to conceal blemishes, dark circles, or any imperfections to the skin. It usually is one shade lighter than an individual's skin tone. Conclear usually comes in a pot for heavy consistency, a tube for medium coverage or a wand for light application. Concealer also can be used as a base for your eye shadow application. National makeup artist Olga Molrales advises that concealers should be yellow based, not pink or beige. Yellow neutralizes dark shadows and any red blemishes on the face. Some concealers even have a green tint to neutralize a severe red, blotchy complexion. Do not worry—you will not look jaundiced!

Base—Base is the foundation for makeup application. There are many types of makeup bases; however, most people in television seem to prefer pancake makeup, oil-based cream foundations (either available in a pot or in a tube) or dual-application powders. Over-the-counter liquid foundations are not recommended because they do not provide good coverage. The key is to smoothe out the skin tone, diminishing any imperfections. In addition, the optimum look must have a matte finish. In simple terms, a matte look has a satin, buffed finish as opposed to a glossy, shiny appearance. If any surfaces are not dull in a TV studio, including the face, the lights will cause a distracting reflection. The dual-application makeup is the foundation of choice in TV because it is a base and a powder in one compact. You have the option to wet the base or to use it dry. Coverage is excellent with this product as is the ability to achieve a matte look. With any foundation, always select a base color that is one shade darker than your skin tone.

Blush—Most men and women should wear blush on television. Otherwise, individuals develop that pasty corpse-like look. The trick with blush is in the application. A general rule to follow is never to put cream on top of powder because you literally will create a paste-like look versus a finished, matte look. Powder on top of powder is great, along with powder on top of cream. Obviously, men should use blush with discretion to create a natural look.

Brushes—Blending is crucial in makeup application, and brushes allow for you to do this. Morales believes that nothing is more important than a set of high-quality makeup brushes—avoid drug-store quality. Beauty supply shops can advise you on the various product lines. McCoy says that some of her colleagues even buy brushes from artists' supply stores. Keep in mind that a set of brushes can be very expensive; shop around for a quality set within your price range. Morales also advises keeping your brushes clean with shampoo or liquid soap as necessary.

Lipstick and Liner—A "must have" for women. We recommend wearing a matte color. Avoid glosses or frosts because they tend to reflect light. Most lipsticks will indicate on the packaging whether or not they are matte or gloss. Also, women will want to avoid bizarre colors such as purple or fire red—you do not want to draw too much attention. Liner is usually one shade darker than the lipstick. Once the lips are lined, Morales lightly fills the entire lip with liner, creating more staying power for her clients. Liner tends to be beneficial because it stops the lipstick from bleeding, along with defining the contour of the lips. Men should only consider lipstick if they have lips with little color. Be careful! A brick color is usually very natural, and you would not want to apply it directly from the tube because you will look like a man wearing lipstick! Put a little on the index finger and blend over the lips. Most importantly, always check your teeth for lipstick smudges. You can apply a little petroleum jelly to your teeth to keep the lipstick from sticking.

Eye shadow—People tend to be confused about shadow because there are so many colors from which to choose. Many makeup artists suggest using two shades of brown to create a natural look. The base on the lid should be light, and the crease should be dark to set the eyes. Again, blending is the key.

Eyebrow Pencil—Use eye shadow to fill in the eyebrows. Eyebrow pencil for the eyebrows is sometimes too harsh for the cameras, but it does make wonderful eyeliner. Clear brow gel, sometimes found at drug stores, works well for men if the eyebrows are unruly; however, it is difficult to find. In addition, some makeup artists may want to trim or pluck your brows if necessary.

Eyeliner—A *soft* black pencil is excellent to line most eyes. Stay away from liquid liner because, once again, it can be too harsh and it is difficult to apply!

The exception to using black pencil would be if you have blond or red hair. In this case you would want to use a dark or medium brown pencil. Remember to blend the pencil. This is where rubber tips on the ends of the pencils are great because they help blend the line, creating a softer look.

Mascara—The rule with mascara is the same as for eyeliner regarding the choice of colors. Please, no blue shades! Find a brand that does not leave clumps on the eyelashes.

Powder—Powder is a must! It is probably the most important item to have if you are going to be in front of the camera. Have blotting or rice powder papers on hand if you dislike powder. A translucent powder is a good choice because it does not have a base color. Morales offers this tip: When lining your lips and the eyes with pencil, be sure to set your liner with powder. This keeps the liner from bleeding or smudging on your eyes or lips. For your eyes, you can take an applicator and dip the tip in dark brown shadow, going over the eyeliner to hold it in place. Remember, the basic function of powder is to cut down on the shine and prevent smudging. A prominent TV producer pointed out that she could tell amateur productions from professional programs quite easily. Basically, the amateur productions had spokespeople whose skin was noticeably shiny. So, do not forget the powder!

Makeup and Lighting

Understanding the key elements of lighting is imperative when applying makeup. McCoy finds that even with minimal lighting, the only base that really gives a matte finish is a pancake base. Lights can create shine and too much shadow. Sometimes they even "wash" you out so that your face looks extremely pale. The rule is to do enough air checks (looking at yourself on tape) so that you can adapt to the lighting, especially if you do outdoor shoots. Sometimes, in a freelance situation, you will not have the luxury of having enough time to adapt to the environment.

Here are some basic terms and rules that you should become familiar with concerning lighting:

Key lights—This light is the main source of illumination. A producer will adjust this light to enhance your appearance.

Gels—These are plastic sheets of color placed over lights to set mood. You may have to adjust your makeup application depending on the colors of gels selected. For example, a red gel would require talent to apply less blush because it provides enough red color.

Diffusion—This is material placed over lights to soften their intensity. It sometimes is used for people with bad acne or wrinkles. Diffusion visually softens the appearance, diminishing some of the demarcations on the skin.

Brightness—Never look up at the studio lights. Allow yourself time to acclimate to the lighting environment to avoid squinting.

Outdoor lighting—Generally, the sun is the main

source of illumination. For television live shots, a light or reflector may be used to throw light on your face. Many producers want you to face the sun to illuminate you. Most producers will avoid shooting between 11:00 a.m. and 1:00 p.m. because the sun is directly above you and will cause harsh and unnatural shadows such as the appearance of deep-set eyes and more pronounced hairlines. Also, nose shadows would be cast over the mouth, defeating the purpose of even wearing lipstick and liner.

Shopping

While providing you with a checklist is helpful, confusion usually sets in when people have to go to the store to buy makeup products. There are three types of stores to visit:

- Theatrical makeup stores
- Department stores
- Discount and drug stores

First, you can visit a theatrical makeup store (sometimes referred to as a costume shop). Always check the shades, especially with makeup bases. Some clerks will ask you to try the makeup on the top of your hand. There is a problem with this approach because most people's hand color is different from their face color. Test the colors on the jaw line. This method will probably provide a more accurate shade. Usually in these types of stores, you will find oil-based products or pancake makeup; however, blushes and eye color usually are provided in a powder base. Most theatre makeup products are moderately priced.

The next option for makeup shopping is the department store. You may find the clerks helpful, but the products will be more expensive. Remember, sales people make a commission by selling the most they possibly can to you. However, you may enjoy a visit to the cosmetic counter because you get an individualized consultation. Many males appreciate having someone "walk" them through the product selection. There is no problem with this choice, but remember what you need and resist what you do not have to purchase.

Perhaps the most reasonable place to shop is a discount store or a drug store. There are many products displayed at these stores that rival the department store in quality. The challenge is that many items are packaged and not available to sample, but you may save more than 50 percent compared to what you would be paying at the department store! Another challenge is that most sales clerks in discount stores do not necessarily specialize in makeup products. Either way, these stores are the most reasonable in price. Finally, if you still are uncomfortable purchasing makeup products, you can hire a consultant. Broadcast makeup artists usually are listed in the AFTRA (American Federation of Television and Radio Artists) broadcast union book. There should be a local chapter near you. Expect to pay someone a consultant's fee, but it may well be worth the investment. Also, working with a professional artist who is familiar with TV makeup is an excellent way to get basic training for self-application.

People of Color

Many people of color have inquired about appropriate shade choices for makeup and wardrobe. Darlene Mathis, author and expert on beauty consulting for women of color, suggests that color analyses should be multicultural in scope. Diversity should be reflected in color choices whether it is makeup, hair or wardrobe planning.* In addition to makeup specialists, there are color consultants who can work with you to help you decide what your palette should be. As with lighting, makeup colors can enhance your skin tone or wash you out. So, pay close attention to your color palette.

Figures 9 and 10 will serve as a guide for you to apply basic makeup. It is sometimes helpful to use the face sketch to practice. People find it is easier to go through the makeup application process on paper a few times with colored pencils or crayons before attempting to work on their own faces. Remember, even if you cannot sketch well, you do not have to be an artist to put on makeup!

Aging and Cosmetic Surgery

Aging is something we all have to face at some point in our lives. Cameras pick up many details on the face. Unfortunately, fine lines and wrinkles tend to show up on the screen when we do not necessarily want them to. With the advent of high-definition television (HDTV), most demarcations or flaws on the skin will be more noticeable than ever before. This will happen because the lines of scansion will go from 525 to around 1200. In simple terms, your TV picture will become extremely clear, detailing objects as if they were right in your living room.[2]

How do you get rid of unsightly lines or blemishes? First, you should always consult with a plastic surgeon or a dermatologist for cosmetic advice. According to J. Sheldon Artz, MD, renowned plastic surgeon in Cleveland, Ohio, people have 90 seconds to sell themselves. Whether you are a CEO, a news anchor, or a shoe salesperson, appearance is very important. Artz claims that, while cosmetic surgery is an option to maintain that youthful look, nothing replaces a good skin-care program, along with a healthy lifestyle. Products containing Retin A and

---

[*] For more information on makeup, hair or wardrobe planning for people of color, see *Women of Color: The Multicultural Guide to Fashion and Beauty* by Darlene Mathis.

alpha hydroxy help maintain a youthful glow; however, Artz warns his clients not to get caught up in the hype of all the new over-the-counter products claiming to capture the fountain of youth with a "quick fix." Instead, he thinks it is wise to consider visiting a good dermatologist before embarking on any skin-care program.

There are many cosmetic procedures available that intrigue people. Your plastic surgeon or dermatologist can share a multitude of age-defying procedures and products with you. Naturally, you should call on a credible plastic surgeon if your cosmetic needs are more ambitious. Artz suggests applying a good sunscreen and drinking plenty of water to delay the aging process.

Figure 9
Basic Makeup Application for Women

Eyeliner should start at halfway point on bottom, but follow the entire end of the eyelid on top.

Darker shade on crease.

Light shade on eyelid.

Concealer should be one shade lighter than base.

Blush should start slightly above the nose from the center of the eye.

Use lip liner to trace line of lips. Fill in with a lighter shade of lipstick. Blot with tissue and powder so lipstick will not bleed into skin.

Makeup Application Steps

1. Cleanse face
2. Tone with astringent
3. Moisturize face, especially under eyes, and blot face with tissue
4. Put concealer on blemishes (spots) and under eyes to cover dark circles, setting with powder
5. Apply base on entire face, blending downward
6. Apply blush, blending well
7. Put lighter shade of eye shadow on eyelid
8. Put dark shade of eye shadow on crease, blending well
9. Follow with eyeliner, mascara, and eyebrows
10. Fill in entire lip with lip liner and apply lipstick
11. Set entire face with translucent powder, wiping off excess with brush or powder puff

Figure 10

Basic Makeup Application for Men

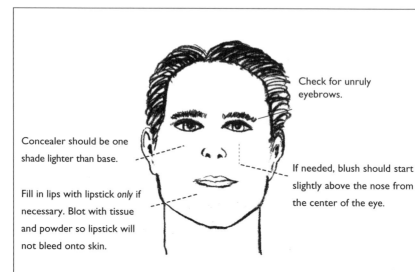

Check for unruly eyebrows.

Concealer should be one shade lighter than base.

If needed, blush should start slightly above the nose from the center of the eye.

Fill in lips with lipstick *only* if necessary. Blot with tissue and powder so lipstick will not bleed onto skin.

Makeup Application Steps for Men

1. Cleanse face
2. Tone with astringent
3. Moisturize face, especially under eyes, and blot face with tissue
4. Put concealer on blemishes (spots) and under eyes to cover dark circles
5. Apply base on entire face, blending downward
6. Apply blush, if needed, blending well
7. Follow with mascara if needed
8. Set entire face with translucent powder, wiping off excess powder from eyebrows and lips
9. Check eyebrows to ensure that they are not unruly

Practice

Though authors rarely encourage readers to photocopy their books, in this case, we strongly suggest you photocopy and enlarge Figures 9 or 10 for practicing your makeup application. The more you practice the makeup-application process, the better you will feel when you apply cosmetics to your own face. Use colored pencils or crayons on these diagrams for practice.

Tip

When you are in makeup, drink beverages with a straw. Your lipstick will stay on much longer if you stay away from drinking out of cups or glasses. Also, applying a little makeup base to your lips before you put on lipstick will provide more staying power.

Key Points

- **Shopping**—Check out theatre makeup supply stores, department stores, discount/drug stores, or consultants to get your supplies (makeup kits).
- **Prepare the skin**—Cleanse, tone, and moisturize your face and eyes. Apply concealer, base, blush and powder, blending well. Define your eyes and lips, and groom, if necessary. Wipe your eyebrows of any excess makeup base smudges. Remember, try to create a natural look.
- **Lighting**—You should have a basic understanding of how you look under different types of

lighting. Experiment so that you can adjust your makeup application accordingly.

- **Cosmetic surgery**—Always consult with a dermatologist about any procedures you may be considering about your face or body. Licensed estheticians are great to work with if you are looking at superficial procedures such as facials, skin peels, and other services. Nevertheless, the safest way to approach skin enhancements should be through a licensed dermatologist or a cosmetic surgeon.

HAIRSTYLES FOR TV

The Look

Over the years, it has been interesting to observe news anchors, talent and company spokespeople dealing with what is considered an "in" hairstyle. It is a battle between what styles are current versus what styles are appropriate for the occasion. Imagine an anchorperson attempting to go from being a dark brunette to a blond. You do not have to be a licensed cosmetologist to guess what would happen. First, it would be a shock to the viewing audience to see the radical change, and they would have difficulty accepting it. Second, the color would be a very unnatural, brassy yellow instead of an attractive blond. While some people may not be overly concerned about how their hair looks, people in front of the camera should be almost obsessive about their style.

Probably the best rule for both men and women to follow is to keep the look conservative. Some people interpret conservative as boring, but you do not want viewers to be so transfixed on your hair that they quit paying attention to what you are saying. You also do not want a long hair style that will get wind blown or droop if it rains. This chapter should give you some guidance on the basics of hairstyles and nail upkeep.

Facial Shapes

The first aspect of selecting a hairstyle that is right for you is to determine the shape of your face. One could say it is like dressing a store-front window—consider the shape of the window before thinking about a design. Use the following chart of facial shapes to help you determine which styles to *avoid*.

Figure 11
Facial Shapes

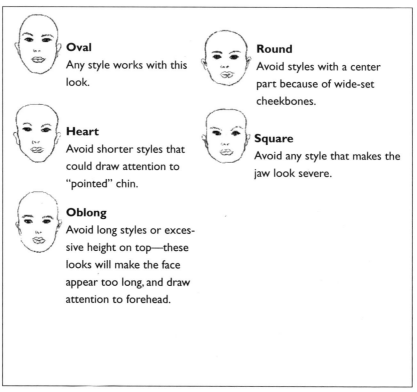

Oval
Any style works with this look.

Round
Avoid styles with a center part because of wide-set cheekbones.

Heart
Avoid shorter styles that could draw attention to "pointed" chin.

Square
Avoid any style that makes the jaw look severe.

Oblong
Avoid long styles or excessive height on top—these looks will make the face appear too long, and draw attention to forehead.

Adapted and modified from Ziggie Cieplinski and Patti Cieplinski, "Styles on Video," NorthCoast News, 1 March, 1994, 5.

Styles

No one wants a boring hairstyle. How do you remain conservative but in "vogue"? Clearly, some haircuts are considered timeless. For example, if you look at photographs since the inception of television, basic styles have been modified. (The same seems to hold true with clothing.) Many people remember the classic "bob cut" that Jackie Kennedy had in the 60s. That style would be acceptable today on television with a few modifications.

There are no hard-set rules when it comes to style. The best advice may be to ask your news director, producer, or whoever might be your superior. As television talent, you should not change your hairstyle at your own discretion. Most news directors, general managers and producers want a consistent look. As an anchor or any other type of talent, you are a station's spokesperson so you must be flexible with your look.

Hair Textures and Products

Once you have considered a style, it may be necessary to modify the look because of the texture of your hair. At this point, a consultation with a licensed stylist is recommended. Sometimes, it may be that you have to use a different product on your hair, rather than modifications, to achieve the desired look. For example, many stylists use a foam mousse on hair instead of gel because the gel weighs fine hair down too much. Another example would be people with coarse, porous hair purchasing a strong permanent solution that will make their hair frizzy, or talent with curls trying to maintain a style designed for hair that is straight by using a hair relaxer.

It is advisable to use professional products from hair salons as opposed to other stores. You will be spending more money, but stylists use the products on your hair to create the look you are trying to achieve. Also, most stylists will know if your hair texture is not adaptable to a certain look. In television news, you may be applying spray or mousse several times in one day, so it is important to use the right product.

Consultations

In most markets, TV stations do not provide hair stylists for their news anchors or guests. This is true for talk shows and most Internet and teleconferencing broadcasts, too. This philosophy does not hold true with other types of video productions where a hair stylist may be provided.

In order to find a good hair stylist, first call your local TV stations and ask to speak with some news anchors or reporters. Ask them who does their hair, especially if you like the style. The next step is to set up a consultation with the stylist. Some higher-priced salons charge for consultations, but many shops will offer you free advice in hopes of earning your business. Let them look at a videotape if you have one available. Again, consider your facial shape and have the stylist give you some options regarding the choice of styles that will work well on camera.

Many news directors prefer male anchors and reporters to have short, neatly groomed hair. Also, men should be clean-shaven or have a well-trimmed mustache. Mustaches should be trimmed so that the hairs are slightly above the lip. A similar standard is true with females regarding their hair length; however, news directors seem to be a little more flexible with female on-air talent concerning their hairstyles. There are, of course, exceptions to these preferences. Some female anchors have wonderful long hairstyles. The key is for the look to be professional and not distract from the news delivery.

Another approach to consider if you are unsure of where to go to seek hair advice is to look through the AFTRA directory under hair or makeup. Always ask whether the stylist has a cosmetology license.

Finally, you might consider computer imaging. This approach to hairstyle shopping was very popular in the early 90s. Once a photo is taken of you, the computer software provides you with several different looks. You choose from a wide selection of looks, and the system provides printouts of how you look in a particular style. You can then take the print to a hairstylist to use as a reference. The cost of such a service varies, but finding a salon that provides this service may be challenging. Check out your local salons for current information on this procedure.

Nails

The same advice for hair applies to fingernails for both men and women. Your nails should be neat and professional. For most women who go in front of the camera, whether it is news or not, a professional length and subdued color choice seem preferable. Men should look into having their nails manicured and buffed.

Nails can create problems on camera. A national spokesperson was called to do a video for a computer corporation. After she was hired to do the role of a computer executive for the corporation, she was told that she would do some head shots of on-camera announcing and voice-over work. She was not worried about her nails being extremely long and painted fire-engine red because they would not be on camera. After one day on the set, the producer told her that the client wanted some B-Roll (cut-away footage, no audio) of her hands at the computer board. The look of horror on the client's face when she gazed down at her vibrant red nails made her realize that most of the executives in the company had more professional-looking nails. Her nails were clearly not acceptable. You do not want your viewers to become distracted by something as simple as nail color. Some news directors *discourage* female anchors from having nails longer than one quarter of an inch over the finger tips. Always keep your nails natural and professional.

Practice
Take some time and work with your hair. See if you can create at least two different styles. Test your different looks on camera.

Tips
Always have hair spray on hand in the event you have "fly-away" hair. Also, watch for sprays that create too much sheen because of the potential reflection from the studio lights.

Key Points

- Determine the shape of your face.
- Look at styles that are professional, along with inquiring at your local TV station as to where the talent get their hair done.
- Consult with a licensed cosmetologist to achieve the desired look.
- Use professional, salon products on your hair.
- Keep nails manicured and at a professional length. No bold polish colors!
- Work with a professional if you are required to wear a wig or a hairpiece.

WARDROBE FOR TV

Unless you get a job as a performer in Hollywood or New York, you probably will not have a wardrobe consultant for a TV shoot. It is very difficult to find people who are skilled in wardrobe consulting for television. When working with sales-clerks, for example, you may have to *coach them* more than they *guide you* in fashion for TV. Some clerks may not know that it is not advisable to wear bold patterns on TV, or that some patterns like small checks and stripes would look to the eyes of the viewer as if they were moving on the TV screen.

There are very few "fashion consultants" in the TV business. An excellent one, however, is Dawn E. Waldrop, nationally recognized speaker, trainer and author and founder of Best Impressions, an image-developing company. Waldrop's approach to wardrobe planning is widely respected. Her program focuses on looking professional, something people really desire when they are called to be on television. If you have a basic understanding of what constitutes a good TV wardrobe, you can go almost anywhere, from exclusive boutiques to consignment shops, to get your clothes. According to Waldrop, style is an important element to consider because your clothing should be an extension of your personality.[1] Here is what Waldrop has to say about style:

STYLE

So often in our careers we try to be what we think others want us to be. Success today is about being authentic—authentic in our words and our dress. You can be your own person, still be comfortable and be your professional best when dressing for the camera.

Key into your own personality which is your preference in textures and designs in your clothes and accessories. Most people will be a combination of two types. These personality types are **natural, classic, dramatic and romantic**. Consider the following descriptions of wardrobe personalities and styles. What works for you as a broadcaster?

NATURAL

Natural men and women prefer a wash and wear hairstyle. They do not want to fuss with their hair. They prefer no pattern in their outfits. If it is a pattern, it would be a soft check, plaid or small dot; however, naturals should take caution because of the camera's sensitivity toward these choices. They like a thicker material and texture. Tweeds and corduroy are favorites of naturals.

While naturals feel more comfortable in

jeans and a cotton shirt with tennis shoes, the reality is that they must conform to a style that is acceptable to a broadcast audience. The natural man prefers a sport coat versus a suit coat. The natural man also likes wearing a dark colored shirt under the sport coat. The woman prefers her suits to be a linen or tweed. Naturals love 100 percent cotton shirts or blouses. The woman prefers little makeup. However, it is important for her to, at least, wear subtle-colored makeup for the camera. For broadcast, the natural man and woman will move somewhat into classic, but never romantic or dramatic.

CLASSIC

Classic style works for any profession, anywhere. In broadcasting, when in doubt, dress *classic*. Classics love this look because it never goes out of style, which saves money. The classic man or woman is conservative and tailored. They prefer a very subtle all-over paisley or small print. The man loves silk ties and the woman loves silk materials. The hairstyle is very controlled. The woman wears makeup that is very fresh and not overstated. Since the classic look is the most conservative, talent may want to build their wardrobe along this line and accessorize with another personality style.

ROMANTIC

Romantic men and women often need to tone down their choices of patterns when dressing for the camera. The romantic man or woman prefers a longer hairstyle. They love soft materials with soft prints like flowered patterns. Women who are romantics usually like the newest colors in makeup and clothes.

They both love jewelry. It pays to be careful because too much jewelry is a distraction on television or the Internet. Even in a suit situation, romantic women and men prefer softer material. Romantic men like suits that have a soft sheen to them. The silk weave in the suit is what creates the sheen. Do not wear these suits on television because the strands reflect the studio lights too much. Compromise and select a blend.

DRAMATIC

Dramatic men and women wear bold prints and bright colors. The dramatic, like the romantic, needs to tone down the color and the patterns for the television cameras. The man loves ties with geometric patterns. The woman loves bold patterns or animal prints. They also like larger accessories.

Dramatic women love to have the nails polished with bright colors and designs. It is important for them to watch the length of their nails and keep the nail color appropriate for the job. The dramatic man prefers the double-breasted, pointed-lapel suit and his hair slicked back or cut in an angular style. The dramatic woman prefers an angular hair cut, too. If you feel you are a dramatic, just remember to tone it down a bit when you are in front of the camera.

THINGS TO REMEMBER

The key in fashion is not to buy a style that does not fit your personality. For example, if the fashion is very dramatic and you are a natural, do not buy that tie or blouse in the dramatic style. When you wear something that is not you, the television audience can tell. People will not remember whether you were "in style," but they will recall whether you looked professional. As professional broadcasting men and women, you never want any article of clothing or an accessory to take away from your message. Also, be consistent with your style.

So when choosing your wardrobe for television appearances, think about your personality and choose what works best—some people even take a personality test![1] Personality is why you may or may not like an article of clothing or an accessory in your closet. When people say they found a great outfit for you, they have keyed into your personality. When *you* see an outfit in the store and say, "Wow, I love that outfit," *you* have keyed into your personality.*

"Be Your Own Person & Be Your Professional Best." Reprinted with Permission by Dawn Waldrop of Best Impressions®

---

* For more information about wardrobe personality and style, see *Best Impressions: How to Gain Professionalism, Promotion and Profit* by Dawn Waldrop.

Colors

Color is imperative when putting together a wardrobe for TV. Once you have decided on a particular style, be sure your color choices work well for you and the TV environment. Here are some nuggets of information about how certain colors come across to the viewer on television:

> **White**—It is not advisable to wear stark white on TV because it has a tendency to glow or "bloom" on the monitor. You can wear a white blouse as long as it is covered by a different shade of jacket or vest. Still, your best bet is to stay away from stark white unless a producer asks for the color.
>
> **Black**—This color is fine on TV, but make sure you add an accent color. A black outfit sometimes comes across looking too severe. And if you are fair, black can wash out your skin tone.
>
> **Red/Green**—While red and green are considered good choices, often the cameras make reds look orange, and some green colors come across more blue. Cameras react differently to color choices. The best rule is to ask a producer if there are color preferences.
>
> **Colored patterns**—Again, stay away from patterns or strange designs such as stripes, checks or loud swirls; they create the illusion of movement. Obviously, your viewers will not be paying attention to you. Instead, they will be focusing on your clothing.

Backdrops

When you are thinking about color choices with your wardrobe, you always must discern the color of the TV studio backdrop. For example, imagine if the backdrop were in black and an anchor wore a stunning black-and-red suit one day to the set. If by chance one sleeve of the suit was red and the other was black, the appearance might be of a one-armed woman! The black sleeve would blend into the backdrop, and all the viewers would notice would be a hand flailing about. Most producers prefer blue as the background of choice because of its contrast with skin tones.[2] Therefore, bright blues usually do not make good wardrobe choices.

Chroma-Key is another thing to inquire about if you are going to be on a studio set. Chroma-Key is a method of superimposing an image over a specific color background on a wall. If you step in front of the wall, and you are wearing the same color, you will blend into the image. Chroma-Key is often used when people are doing the weather during a newscast. Usually the weather people are in front of a blank colored wall, looking off to the side at a monitor so they know where they are pointing. If the wall is green, they should not wear green on the set. The key is to wear a contrasting color. Always assess your environment before making wardrobe choices.

Fabrics and Textures

Fabric choices and textures of clothing are the next items on your list of concerns. The philosophy on this subject is to focus on your lifestyle, as mentioned earlier in this chapter, and on the studio environment. If you are a reporter, chances are you should stay away from fabrics like linen because of its tendency to wrinkle. Reporters often are required to be live at the scene. What if you have been in a car for a long period of time or on location? Your clothes probably are going to wrinkle. Also, people in front of the camera must be careful to avoid spilling anything on their clothes.

Some TV people bring large bibs and aprons along for this reason, or they wear different clothing when they eat their meals. Be careful of this practice because there is always the chance of makeup smearing onto your clothing when you remove it or put it back on, unless the clothing has buttons or zips up the front for easy removal. A better idea is to have several outfits available in case of an unfortunate circumstance like coffee spilling onto your egg-shell-colored suit or your pale yellow tie. Industrial-strength spot removers are good to tuck away in your office drawer or glove compartment. Waldrop suggests women carry three extra pairs of stockings in their cars in case of a hosiery run. The following list should provide you with some fabrics to *avoid* because of their lack of practicality in a TV person's environment or lifestyle:

> **Linen**—This fabric wrinkles too much.
>
> **Silk**—A lightweight fabric that works well for women's blouses, but be careful because the material stains easily and can be expensive to dry-clean.
>
> **Satin**—This material is very shiny for the camera and far too glamorous (unless you are portraying a character in an environment where satin would be appropriate). Also, satin can get quite warm, especially if you are under the studio lights.
>
> **Beaded material/Sequins**—Stay away from this look, along with metallic-looking material because of the reflection of the studio lights. Again, this is too distracting, and people will not listen to what you are saying.
>
> **Chiffon/Lace**—Another pitfall for talent. Chiffon is too sheer, and lace can be excessive if you are wearing too much. An exception

would be lace piping around a collar, for example.

Cotton—We do not recommend 100 percent cotton. This material wrinkles and will shrink too much.

Good Fabric Choices

Polyester/cotton blends—This choice is excellent because you get the crisp look of cotton but the wrinkle-free benefit of polyester.

Rayon—This blend is a favorite in the TV industry because it is easy to clean and keep up.

Tweed—Tweed blends are excellent, but make sure they do not have bold patterns.

Other blends—Currently, there are so many fabric blends that it would take too many pages to list the selections. Remember to consider your environment, lifestyle and image you are trying to convey. Additional questions to address are: Do you have time to wash and iron your clothing? Can you afford dry cleaning? Will the fabric fray if you wear a brooch on your lapel? Will stains easily be removed from your fabric choice? How warm or cool will the environment be where you are taping?

Fabric textures are an extension of your personality; however, there is another practical element to consider. For example, certain fabrics tend to rustle when people move their arms. You may be stopped in the middle of a shoot because of microphone distortion. For instance, if you wear a crepe or a taffeta dress, the fabric would scrape against the microphone, creating an unusual sound. So, think about the look you are trying to convey, but also contemplate how your choices affect your entire presentation.

Accessories

There is no doubt that accessories can make a look complete or tear it apart on camera. Utterback's basic advice to her clients is to avoid anything that might distract from your face by calling attention to the accessory. Large, dangling earrings are a great example of what *not* to wear on camera.

Women can expand their wardrobe by simply adding a scarf or a decorative pin to their ensembles. Men should stock up on ties because a different tie can make the same suit jacket look entirely different. Remember that the same holds true for accessories as for fabric textures—make sure you do not add something that will get in the way of your microphone. We have provided a list of recommended accessories, detailing the pros and cons with each choice. In addition, you will find some tips on scarf tying and a chart for eyeglass shopping. Eyeglasses are considered accessories for both men and women (see Figure 12).[3]

Accessory List

> **Scarves and Belts**—Scarves are a must for every woman's wardrobe. You really can stretch your budget when you purchase scarves. With a scarf, the same black dress you wore one day can completely change the next. Practice some of the suggestions in this text, and visit department stores because they often have scarf-tying booklets on hand to distribute in the accessories department (see Figures 13 and 14). Belts also can tie a garment together. Make sure you recognize the difference between casual belts and dress belts. Do not wear an inappropriate belt.
>
> **Ties**—Men truly can make a statement about their personalities with tie choices. Again, reflect on what type of personality you have and

Figure 12
Eyeglasses

The Round Face

Best Bets: Cat's eyes and rectangles. Try a few that extend beyond the face. Avoid: Circular frames, which will make your cheeks look fuller.

The Oblong Face

Best Bets: Upward curves, rectangles, cat's eyes with squared bottoms. Avoid: Anything that sits too low on the face and frames that extend over the side of the face.

The Heart-Shaped/Triangular Face

Best Bets: Aviator styles that are thicker at the top than at the bottom, ovals, anything straight across the top and rounded at the bottom. These Styles will give your face balance. Avoid: Angular frames and cat's eyes.

The Square Face

Best Bets: Frames that dip slightly below cheekbones. Rounded, oval or aviation frames will balance your squared edges and soften lines. Avoid: Frames that are squared off, top or bottom.

The Oval Face

Best Bets: You can handle almost any type of frame as long as the overall "look" suits you. Avoid: Anything your common sense guides you away from.

Figure 13
Scarves

Faux Bow

Take an oblong scarf and make a knot in center. Place knot in front of neck, crossing both ends behind neck. Bring both ends back to front, putting ends in knot at opposite directions.

Cowl

Take a square scarf and fold into a triangle with the point in front. Bring ends behind neck, crossing to return and tie both ends in front. Take point of scarf and tuck in behind knot.

Adapted and modified from "Scarf Tying: Creative Hot-To's," *Accessories Magazine*.

Figure 14

Scarves, continued

Ascot

Take a square scarf and fold oblong. Bring ends behind neck, returning to front. Flip one end over the other. Can be worn off to the side.

Oblong

Take an oblong scarf and place center in front of neck. Bring ends behind neck, crossing and returning to front.

Figure 15
Jewelry

It is important to wear accessories to create a professional look. Notice how a necklace & earrings frame the face. A scarf or pin could be used instead of the necklace, but create a finished, framed look. Make certain that any accessories you wear are "easy to read." This means they should be large enough to see and not complex. The viewer should not spend time figuring out what the accessory is, such as a small cat pin or a scarf with drawings on it. Your accessories should draw the viewers' eyes to your face.

the image you are trying to get across. Watch for wild patterns because of the distraction element. Waldrop recommends the length of a man's tie should meet the middle of the belt buckle. Avoid going above or below the belt buckle.

Jewelry—Please be careful! Too much jewelry can come across as unprofessional, and it can become distracting. Earrings are important for women because they help frame the face (see Figure 15). Make sure your earrings do not dangle, however. You would not want to report on an impending, violent storm and have your viewers miss a warning because they were paying attention to your earrings. A good rule of thumb is to have earrings larger than a dime but smaller than a quarter. Also, make a note that shiny gold or silver jewelry often reflects the studio light. Luckily, many stores offer brushed gold or silver pieces of jewelry. Gems such as diamonds can provide you with similar problems if you are wearing too many.

Necklaces can enhance any outfit, but beware of dangling chains because of the potential for them to brush against the microphone. A necklace should be large enough to make a visual statement, but it should be right at the neck so that it will not cause problems with the microphone. Watches are excellent accessories, but make sure your time piece coincides with your look, whether it is casual or dressy.

Shopping

While working with someone like Dawn Waldrop is the preferred wardrobe-planning recommendation, that is not always an option. Some cities just do not have someone with TV basics and a flair for wardrobe. By using the guidelines in this chapter, you should be able to comfortably work with store clerks. You may have to coach them a little, but having another set of eyes work with you when planning a wardrobe is beneficial.

Everyone knows that different stores demand different prices for clothing. Naturally, price is always one concern to think about. Many students and beginning broadcasters shop at consignment shops to find reasonable prices. As long as garments are well cared for, there is no reason why you should not consider consignment clothing. The most important thing to remember is to stay away from fads because they quickly become outdated. Also, you do not need to pack your closet full of clothes. Many TV anchors think their wardrobe should consume most of their paychecks. Even though you need to have different looks if you appear on TV regularly, an excessive wardrobe is not necessary. Consider outfits that are interchangeable and reasonably timeless so you can get the most out of your wardrobe. And remember to accessorize to create multiple looks. Also, executives may want to have a couple of TV outfits on hand at the office in the event they are called to go on camera with short notice.

For these reasons, the long-term cost savings might outweigh the expense of seeking a consultant. However, Waldrop is a firm believer in personal image consultations to learn what colors, styles, textures and subtle patterns would suit you best. Also, these consultations allow you to address accessories and grooming techniques. Once you are comfortable with your approach, you could save thousands of dollars. In addition, you never will have that dilemma of whether you should have worn something else.

Alterations

It is important that your clothes fit well for television. McCoy once had a student in class who would wear a suit jacket with sleeves that were too long. He looked like a little boy dressed in a man's suit jacket. Alterations would have solved the problem immediately at a low cost. Even the most expensive clothing can look terrible if it is not altered. Waldrop also advises to make sure the clerks measure *both* arms and legs because one tends to be longer than the other. Make sure you put the outfit back on when the alterations are complete to be sure they are correct.

Practice
Take a look at your wardrobe. How can you expand it with accessories like scarves, belts and ties? Practice expanding your ensembles.

Tip
Avoid wearing clothing without an appropriate place to hide the cord of a lavalier microphone. If you have on just a turtleneck or cowl sweater it can be difficult. The microphone has to be attached onto a lapel, a tie or a buttonhole of a shirt or blouse. Suits *without* lapels are great as long as you have something on which to attach your microphone.

Key Points

- **Style**—Remember to contemplate your personality when building your wardrobe. This decision will affect everything from color choices to fabric options.

- **Color**—Remember not to wear stark white on camera. Also, check with producers to see if certain colors are problems for their cameras. Another question to ask is what color backdrop the studio has available. Think about what colors in your wardrobe would contrast well. In addition, make sure you avoid wild patterns, stripes, checks and large designs on TV because they create the illusion of movement.
- **Fabrics/Textures**—Watch out for fabrics that reflect the light or are distracting to the viewer. Think about microphone interference, too. Remember your environment.
- **Accessories**—Learn to properly accessorize your wardrobe. You will save money, and you can be very creative about your image. Use the guides in this text to start.
- **Shopping**—Your budget should not prevent you from having a complete wardrobe. Consignment shops are an option for people on limited budgets. Be creative and versatile when planning a wardrobe. It is well worth the money if you can afford an image consultant.

BROADCAST VOICE

When anyone is considering a career as a broadcaster or is asked to appear on television or the Internet, one of the first considerations is the voice. Voice draws the viewer in and motivates the viewer to look at the screen. This is true whether you are an executive appearing as a guest on a business show, a doctor talking on the Internet, a manager teleconferencing, or a network television anchor or reporter. Your voice is the first thing people are aware of, and it is what carries your message.

Basic knowledge about breathing, producing sound, resonating sound and shaping sound into words is essential for good vocal production. And if you plan to use your voice on the air, it is also necessary for you to develop respect for your voice and keep it healthy. To make sound, you are using two tiny pieces of muscle and ligament in your throat (your vocal folds). If anything happens to these vocal folds, your voice will suffer. A good voice for broadcasting is one that is healthy and enhances meaning. You need to do everything possible to protect your voice and keep it working well for you.

Think of the voice as an instrument. Not many concert

pianists would abuse their fingers or ballet dancers their legs, but many people abuse their voices daily by smoking, shouting, or continuing to talk when hoarse. It is important to consider all aspects of voice to keep it healthy.

For your voice to work effectively, relaxation is the key. Because the voice depends on various muscles in the body, it reflects the degree of tension a person is feeling. Stress affects all muscle tone, including posture, respiration and voice control. A tense body usually means a tense voice. Keeping your body relaxed and your life in balance will actually help your voice on the air.* When you are appearing on television, it is not a luxury to take good care of yourself; it is a necessity. You should consider exercising daily, eating healthy foods, scheduling regular facials and even getting a massage as part of what it takes to do your job well.

Breathing

Whether you are a broadcaster or a corporate executive, proper breathing can help break the tension that builds as our workday progresses. The breath can be your best ally. It revitalizes the body while calming the emotions and bringing clarity to the mind. And since the breath provides the energy for speech, it can determine the success or failure of your delivery.

The most important muscle for breathing is the diaphragm. The diaphragm is one of the strongest muscles in the body. It is a large sheet-like muscle that separates the thoracic cavity from the abdominal cavity (see Figure 16).

The action of the diaphragm is what allows us to breathe naturally. In its resting state, the diaphragm muscle is dome-shaped (see Figure 17). When we inhale with the diaphragm,

---

* For more information about how to combat stress, see BROADCASTER'S SURVIVAL GUIDE by Ann S. Utterback, Ph.D. (See order information at the end of this book).

this large, sheet-like muscle contracts and flattens out. As it flattens, it moves downward. The ribs flex upward at the same time. The effect of this is to increase the size of the thoracic cavity (see Figure 18).

As you inhale, the diaphragm forces the abdominal area to protrude because of the pressure on the stomach, liver, spleen and other organs beneath it. This movement of the abdominal area makes diaphragmatic breathing easy to monitor. How can you tell if you are breathing with your diaphragm? With a good abdominal-diaphragmatic breath, you feel and see expansion in the stomach area as well as all around the back. The lower chest area may expand as much as 2 ½ inches.

Abdominal-diaphragmatic breathing is one of the best ways to maintain a healthy voice. If the diaphragm and abdominal muscles are doing the work during inhalation and exhalation, there is less tension in the voice. Voice coaches often notice that when many of their beginning clients take a breath, their

Figure 16
Oral and Nasal Cavities

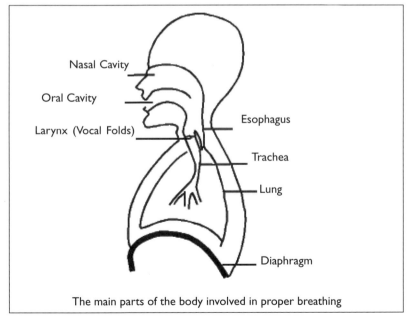

Nasal Cavity

Oral Cavity

Larynx (Vocal Folds)

Esophagus

Trachea

Lung

Diaphragm

The main parts of the body involved in proper breathing

Increase of Volume of Thorax with Inhalation

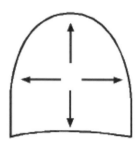

Figure 17
Rib cage before inhalation

Figure 18
Rib cage after inhalation

shoulders rise up. We have all been taught to tuck in our tummies and expand our chests. This results in clavicular (upper chest) breathing that causes the shoulders to rise during inhalation and increases muscular tension in the neck. Clavicular breathing produces a higher vocal pitch when speaking and poor breath support.

To feel abdominal-diaphragmatic breathing, try some of these simple exercises:*

- Sit forward in a chair and put your elbows on your knees. Breathe normally and focus attention on the location of the movement. If you are breathing with the abdominal-diaphragmatic muscles, you should feel movement in your stomach, around your sides, and possibly across your back.
- Stand and bend from the waist at a 90-degree angle, letting your arms and head hang relaxed. Keep your knees slightly flexed. Re-

main in this position until you can feel your abdominal-diaphragmatic breathing.

• Lie down on your back on the floor or a bed. Place your right hand on your chest and your left hand on your abdomen. Notice that you can keep your right hand still while your left hand rises and falls with the breath. Once you have experienced this movement, try placing a book on your abdomen and watch it move up and down as you breathe correctly from the diaphragm.

The diaphragm and abdominal muscles give us both the ability to take in a large volume of air and the ability to control our exhalation of that air. This ability is called *breath support*. With proper breath support, you can produce a strong, confident voice. To check your breath support, inhale with the abdominal-diaphragmatic breath and exhale producing an "ah" sound at a normal conversational level. Time yourself as you exhale your "ah." You should be able to exhale that sound for 20 to 30 seconds without running out of air. If you cannot reach that time, practice each day and try to add a second at a time until you can sustain your exhalation longer.

To improve breath support, a standing posture is recommended for all on-air work. When you are in a seated position, the abdominal area is pushing up into the dome of the diaphragm. When you are standing, the abdominal area is free to expand all around the body. If you must sit, as in an interview situation, sit erect and do not let your back touch the chair. This will give you the best position for good breathing.

---

* More vocal exercises are available on the cassette tape, *Broadcast Voice Handbook: Vocal Exercises* by Ann S. Utterback, Ph.D., produced by Bonus Books and the Radio-Television News Directors Association. You can also find exercises in the text of *Broadcast Voice Handbook*.

Phonation

Breathing alone cannot produce speech. In order for sound to be produced, the air from the lungs must be altered to create sound waves. This is called phonation. When we speak, we alter the air in several ways, but the most important alteration involves the vocal folds. The vocal folds are folds of muscle and ligaments that are located within the larynx. To produce sound, air is exhaled up from the lungs. A fluttering effect happens at the vocal folds as they alternately block the air and let it pass through, which creates sound waves (see Figure 19).

It is easy to feel your vocal folds working. Slide your fingers down the front of your neck until you reach your larynx or Adam's apple, which will feel like a protrusion directly beneath your chin. You are feeling the thyroid cartilage, which is a shield-like structure that protects the vocal folds. With your fingers on your larynx, make a sustained "e" sound, and you will feel vibrations. Swallow and feel the larynx rising up in the throat. Yawn and you will feel the larynx moving downward. All of this movement is controlled by an intricate system of muscles in your throat.

Vocal Health

Taking care of your throat and producing sound correctly are the keys to maintaining a healthy voice. Numerous health problems can affect the larynx and the vocal folds. These problems range from a fairly innocuous sore throat to laryngeal cancer. The voice lets us know fairly quickly if there is something wrong in the throat. Pain, hoarseness and a persistent feeling of a lump in the throat are all signs of a problem. Fortunately, there are many things you can do to protect the throat and vocal folds.

Figure 19
The Vocal Folds

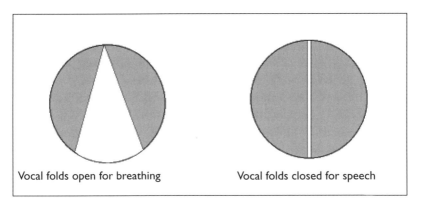

Vocal folds open for breathing   Vocal folds closed for speech

Take hoarseness seriously. Remember that the voice is produced by two delicate pieces of tissue, and abuse of these tissues can cause permanent damage. Utterback has heard horrifying stories from clients about bad advice news directors and other reporters have given them. One of her clients said that she not only was encouraged to go on the air when hoarse, but was told that shouting with a hoarse voice would lower her pitch. Bad advice like this can easily end a person's career. Having healthy vocal folds should be a top priority, and hoarseness is always a sign that the voice is not working properly.

One of the most harmful activities for the voice is smoking. The evidence is overwhelming and irrefutable that smoking damages the vocal mechanism. It is not even a gamble. If you smoke, the odds are that you will develop vocal problems that can range from persistent hoarseness to laryngeal cancer. Do not risk any of these by smoking. If you take your profession seriously, you will not do something that you know will affect your performance and put your career and your life at risk.

Straining the voice in any way has a harmful effect on the vocal folds. Coughing and throat clearing cause the most common vocal abuse. These activities are the result of tremendous air pressure being built up under the vocal folds and expelled, forcing the folds to vibrate explosively. This can cause swelling and may lead to the development of polyps or nodules on the vocal folds.*

One food group that makes most people clear their throats and cough is dairy products, which establish a condition in the throat that is conducive to the development of mucus. If you like to drink milk in the morning or have cereal for breakfast, you may find yourself clearing your throat all morning. Save the consumption of dairy products for after your on-air work if you find they contribute to coughing or throat clearing.

Excessive mouth breathing can dry out the throat. It is appropriate to breathe through your mouth when you are talking. At other times, breathing should be through the nose so that the air can be filtered, warmed, and moisturized before it goes into the laryngeal area. If you have any blockage in the nose that causes mouth breathing, contact a physician. In addition, you should avoid breathing through your mouth when you are asleep. Sleeping on your back will often cause mouth breathing. Since this sleeping posture may cause back pain as well, it should be avoided. Sleeping on your side with your mouth closed is best.

If you have a stuffy nose from a cold or sinus infection, antihistamines will help open a blocked nasal cavity, but they accomplish this by drying out the tissues. If the nose is dried out, the throat is also. When you have a cold it is difficult to avoid drying the throat since you will most likely be breathing through your mouth if you do not take something. This is one of the reasons why it is so important to drink plenty of liquids and inhale steam when you have cold symptoms. Also, take single-symptom medications to treat your most prominent symptom each day. Stay away from antihistamines since they have an excessive drying effect on the vocal tract. Take them only when prescribed by a physician for allergies. A single-symptom decongestant is a better choice. Avoid multi-symptom cold medications since they often include medications you do not need.

---

* See *Broadcast Voice Handbook* for a more complete discussion of these vocal problems.

One important chemical that takes water out of the body by acting as a diuretic on the kidneys is caffeine (or technically xanthine, which includes the chemicals in tea and cocoa). One cup of coffee will not have a tremendous effect, but coffee combined with other sources of caffeine can contribute to fluid loss. You should keep your caffeine consumption at around 200 milligrams per day, which is about two small cups of coffee or four sodas.

The best way to combat the drying effects of caffeine and environmental factors is by drinking as much water as possible. You should try to drink at least one-half your body weight in ounces of water per day. This may seem like an excessive amount, but this is what your body needs. It is much healthier to keep a mug filled with water on your desk rather than coffee.

Resonance

When people think of the classic "deep pipes" of a television or radio announcer, they are thinking of the effect resonance has on the voice. Once sound waves are produced at the vocal folds, they are augmented and enriched as they pass through the resonating cavities (see Figure 16: Oral and Nasal Cavities). Resonance not only gives us each a different voice, but it also allows our voices to be heard. If sound waves were not resonated, they would produce a faint sound barely audible to the human ear.

Listening to several stations at news time reveals voices that vary in pitch and resonance. Luckily, broadcasting no longer demands the booming voices it did in the past. The main consideration in today's market is to have a relaxed, well-resonated voice that enhances meaning. Artificially lowering pitch for an on-air voice is distracting to the listener and harmful to the vocal mechanism.

There are other vocal characteristics that can be distracting, and many of these are the result of problems with reso-

nance. Nasality is produced by an excessive amount of nasal resonance, which produces the classic nasal voice. Denasality is too
little nasal resonance. This is the sound you have when your nose
is blocked as it often is with a cold. A thin voice and a throaty
voice result from problems with placement of sound waves in the
mouth. All of these problems can be improved by working with a
voice specialist.

Articulation

A healthy, well-resonated sound is worthless for speech if it is not
articulated into words. Words in our language are made up of
phonemes (individual sounds) that combine to give meaning. We
use our articulators to shape sound waves into phonemes (see
Figure 16: Oral Cavity).

The expressions, "lazy tongue" or "lazy mouth" indicate the importance of flexibility for good articulation. If the articulators are sluggish, it is difficult to articulate sounds clearly.
Frequently this is also referred to as "sloppy speech." Sometimes
this is adequate in relaxed conversation, but poor articulation is
never acceptable for broadcasting.

Listening to broadcasters, you will hear omissions of
phonemes to greater or lesser degrees. Some will have very pre-
cise deliveries while others omit some sounds. Intelligibility,
credibility and precision of pronunciation are all linked. For this
reason, working to pronounce words correctly on television is essential.

Precision of pronunciation can be improved by practicing. Mark the ending plosive sounds (/t/ /d/, /p/ /b/, /k/ /g/) in
some printed material with a highlighter or underline them.
Once they are marked, practice reading the sentences exaggerating the pronunciation of the endings until you can read them
comfortably.

Here are some sentences to practice right now:

```
The boy hit the ball with the bat.
Bob got the job before he left on
his trip.
Check the log to see if Brad paid.
```

Conversely, another concern is to avoid "popping P's." Microphones are very sensitive to the "P" sound and the "B" sounds at the beginning of sentences. Sometimes backing away from the microphone can help as well as making a conscious effort not to push out so much air for these sounds. McCoy tells her students to say "put" one time, really exaggerating the "P." The second time do not push as much air out, softening the "P" sound. You also may see a microphone covered with a "plosive" screen to diminish the hard "P" and "B" sounds.

Tongue twisters can help warm-up the articulators. Repeating the phrase "You see Oz" or "fat lazy cat" in an exaggerated manner stretches the mouth and jaw. Any activity that brings more openness and flexibility into the mouth area can help improve articulation. It is also helpful to keep a list of commonly mispronounced words to practice daily.

Knowing the fundamentals of vocal production is only the beginning of the process of voice improvement. Breathing correctly and keeping a healthy and relaxed throat are the first steps in improving broadcast voice. But just as pianists or dancers must practice daily to maintain their skills, broadcasters must learn that voice improvement is a lifetime pursuit. Maintaining a good broadcast voice takes hours of practice and a lifetime of respect.

Tips

Knowing how your voice works and taking care of it is imperative for good vocal production. Think of the intricate system that allows us to speak and take steps on a daily basis to keep your throat and voice healthy.

> **Practice**
> Monitor how much water you drink every day for a week. Use a tall bottle of water which is around 50 ounces. Fill that up in the morning and try to drink at least that much water during the day.

Key Points

- The voice is produced by an incredibly intricate system of muscles and ligaments.
- For the voice to work effectively, it must be respected—no yelling, excessive coughing, smoking or throat-clearing.
- Drink half your body weight in ounces of water every day.
- Use abdominal-diaphragmatic breathing.
- Reduce your stress level so that it will not negatively affect your voice.
- Warm up the muscles of your mouth before going on air so that you can articulate effectively.

SOUNDING CONVERSATIONAL

When appearing on television or the Internet, you want to be a comfortable communicator and not an announcer. The phrase "comfortable communicator," however, poses two common problems. First, you have to be comfortable. If you are just beginning to do broadcasting work, you may find that your nervousness makes it very difficult for you to feel, look and sound comfortable. And secondly, if you are not familiar with reading copy or talking to a camera, you may find it is difficult to communicate your message well. After all, talking to a camera is not something most people do on a regular basis. So being a "comfortable communicator" is not easy.

We are all familiar with basic communication in everyday life. We learn at an early age that when we say something we usually receive feedback. If a baby cries, for example, the baby knows someone will respond. As we get older, we observe people giving us both verbal and nonverbal feedback every time we speak (see Figure 20). If you are telling a friend about your last vacation, for example, that friend probably will say things like, "Really," or your friend might smile and nod. This feedback helps you adjust your delivery to the situation. Imagine if your friend began looking at his watch or yawning. You would change the way you were talking to him to regain his interest. His feedback would help you make the right choices to sound conversational.

When you are on camera, you often are left in a situation where this feedback is missing. You might be talking directly into a camera or to the wall in a sound booth. Messages are sent out, but no feedback is there to help you make the subtle adjustments needed in stress and intonation to sound conversational. The communication model that we are all so familiar with becomes truncated (see Figure 21).

Script Marking

There are two things you can do to help you achieve a comfortable, conversational style on the air. The first is to spend some time marking your script to aid in your delivery. Whether you are an executive reading a report for a teleconference or a television news anchor giving us the day's news, you need to *verbally underline* the meaning of what you are reading for your listener. Marking your script will help you do this.

Marking your script also forces you to spend some time reading your copy out loud and rehearsing it. No one can do a good job when they read their material on the air for the first time cold. This is called a "rip and read" in the news business, and it is usually the sign of a beginner or a broadcaster who does not have a sense of professionalism. There may be occasional times when a crisis is happening and a broadcaster is being handed news as it is breaking, but this is rare. With that exception, it is your responsibility to carve out the time to read through your copy out loud prior to going on air. This also will give you a chance to be certain that there are no words in the copy that you do not know how to pronounce correctly. Mispronouncing a word in an on-air presentation destroys your

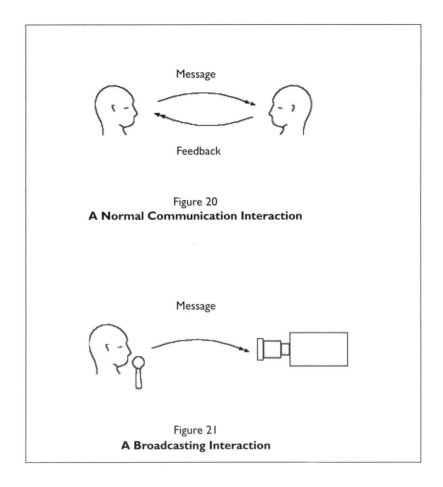

Message

Feedback

Figure 20
A Normal Communication Interaction

Message

Figure 21
A Broadcasting Interaction

credibility. The more time you can spend reading your copy out loud and preparing for your on-air event, the better your delivery will be.

Something as simple as marking where you plan to stop talking and take a breath can help. To find these breath pauses, read your script out loud as if you were talking to a friend. Wherever you stop to take a breath, put a slash mark (/). You can use double slash marks for longer breaths (//), which might occur at periods, and single slash marks for quick breaths that might come at commas or when you need more air within a sentence.

Read these sentences in a conversational manner, and put slash marks where you stop to breathe:

```
Today on Capitol Hill three people
were injured when their car hit the
capitol gates. They were taken to
George Washington University
Hospital where one is listed in
critical condition.
```

You may have found in reading this that you stopped to breathe after "Hill" in the first sentence. Or you may have broken that sentence after "injured." The choice of where to breathe will vary with different readers. The important thing is that you make it sound conversational. The only mistake you can make with a breath pause is to take it at a point that will affect the meaning of the copy. If you paused after "Capitol" you would certainly affect the meaning of the copy. Likewise, if you were reading a sentence and said, "Twenty // million dollars" with a long pause after "twenty," you would affect the meaning of the copy. These are not places we normally would stop to breathe in conversation. Many times when broadcasters have not thought about where they plan to breathe, they find themselves having to take these inappropriate pauses. This is one of the reasons why marking your script can be so helpful.

Once you have marked your breath pauses, look at each group of words between breath pauses. In these groups of words, select what you think are the most important words or the *meaning-laden* words. Meaning-laden words are the words that we must have to understand the story. Once you have selected them, they should outline the story. If all the other words fell off the page, these words would have to remain to let us know what the story is about. In the previous example about Capitol Hill, what do you think the meaning-laden words are?

If you selected "three people," "injured," "car," "capitol gates," "hospital," "one," and "critical," you will have an outline of the meaning of that copy. Those are the words we most likely would emphasize in conversation. You might wonder why certain words like "today" were not selected. Since this is current news of the day, you would not need to stress that word. And do we really need to stress the name of the hospital? We probably do not unless that is a unique aspect of the story. Remember to be judicious in selecting words. Keep your selection to a bare minimum so that you will not end up stressing every word. To check your selection of meaning-laden words, read only your meaning-laden words out loud once you have selected all of them and see if you have an outline of the sentence.

Meaning-Laden Words

Meaning-laden words are not always the nouns and verbs. In the sentence, "The dog was barking loudly which disturbed the neighborhood," the word "loudly" is important. This is an adverb, which is not something you might think would be emphasized. It is important to add the verb to the adverb for it to carry meaning, however, so that the phase "barking loudly" would have to be stressed. This is true of adjectives and adverbs. You have to stress the noun or verb along with them.

Once you have selected your meaning-laden words, think about how you might stress these words in conversation. We often use pitch, for example, to stress a word or phrase in conversation by going up in pitch or down in pitch. We also say words faster or slower. And we say some words more loudly when we want to stress them. All of these are good choices for ways you can change your voice to stress your meaning-laden words.

Utterback suggests that you mark your meaning-laden words in some way so that when you are reading your script you will have some cues to follow.* How you mark the words can be a personal shorthand method you develop. You can use arrows going up or down over the words when you want to change your pitch (inflection). You might circle the words on which you want to increase your volume or you might double underline them. Use

---

* See *Broadcast Voice Handbook* by Ann S. Utterback, Ph.D. for more about a marking system you can use.

any marks that work for you. This will give you an easy way to know that you are stressing words correctly when you read your script. Your marking will aid you as a musical score aids a singer, allowing him or her to concentrate on the words of the song.

The basic stressing method described above (pitch, duration and volume changes) provides a guideline that will give your delivery some inflection, allowing you to sound more conversational on the air. Marking your script lets you superimpose a natural, conversational delivery on what is really a very artificial event. Using this method, you will be able to verbally underline meaning-laden words for your listener just as you do in normal conversation.

It is important to remember that any story or commercial script can be marked in a number of different ways and still be effective. There is no set way to mark just as there is no set way to tell a story in conversation. The choice of what to stress is a personal one. The important thing is that you verbally underline the meaning-laden words, especially in commercial copy because you are trying to promote a product.

It may take weeks or months to get comfortable with a marking process so that your delivery is smooth and does not draw attention to itself. At first, you probably will be very aware that you are following your markings when you stress words. It may sound overdone, but the process eventually should become automatic.

Begin by marking stories from the newspaper or a magazine just to practice your marking method. Once you have marked some copy, read it into an audio recorder so that you can listen to yourself and be certain that you followed your markings. With this practice, you will learn to mark your script and use your voice to enhance meaning with the knowledge that you are emphasizing the correct words in a conversational manner. McCoy suggests to her students in commercial TV that they write their own spots and practice reading them regularly.

Talking To A Person

The second method of sounding conversational is based on the age-old advice that every on-air person has been given—just imagine you are talking to someone. But it may be hard to conjure up an image when you are facing a camera or the wall in a sound booth. Utterback jokes that it is not easy to hallucinate on command. It takes a step-by-step process to create the image. Begin the process by imagining a person. But this is not a vague, nebulous image. Pick a real person with whom you are comfortable talking, someone you can imagine very vividly—a sister, neighbor, cousin. If you think of the audience to whom you will be talking, it should help in this selection. Choosing her 80-year-old grandmother, for example, would not be a good choice for a computer executive who is speaking to her staff in a company video presentation.

We all know how to tell a good story to a friend. We might raise our pitch when we want to stress a word, and we might stretch some words out and say others faster. We do this naturally because of the feedback we get from our friend when we are talking (see Figure 20). Creating a person to talk with helps these same qualities become part of broadcast delivery.

Visualization

The most important thing to remember is that in broadcasting you are always talking with one person as others eavesdrop. Good interpersonal communication sounds like you are talking with just one person.

Some of Utterback's clients even take a photograph of the person into the sound booth or place it on the anchor desk. This helps them keep the listener in mind. The listener is always the most important person in the broadcasting encounter. Vividly creating this person in your mind creates a sense of interpersonal communication.

Once the person has been selected, put that person in a

room where you might normally talk with him or her. Selecting a friend or family member makes it easy to visualize them in the room where they would be watching television or listening to the radio. You might know, for example, that your friend's television is in her kitchen. You can imagine what the room looks like. You can see her sitting at the table, and you might even be able to imagine the smell of the coffee. All these sensual factors help bring this person to life. Or you might imagine a colleague sitting at his desk looking at his computer monitor. You know what his office looks like so as you come to him over the Internet, you can imagine being with him.

We all do this everyday when we talk on the telephone. If we call for airline reservations, for example, we imagine the office the agent is sitting in. We even imagine what the person looks like. Using our imaginations is something we all do well. You need to use this skill whenever you are talking on television. Really see the person or people you have selected and imagine them in the room where they would be listening or watching. This visualization may only take a few seconds, but it will help create a sense of talking with someone.

Visualization or creative imagery like this has been used in sports and theatre for years. Many sports figures spend time imagining they are hitting home runs or making three-pointers. Dancers see themselves leaping effortlessly across the stage. You can use the same skill to create a person. You want to have the feeling that you are talking *with* this person instead of *at* a camera or microphone.

Emotion

Another factor in interpersonal communication is emotion. Emotion plays a significant role in commercial television (commercials, industrials and acting). It is never appropriate for a reporter or an anchor reading the news to editorialize during a straight newscast. Showing emotion in a news story applies only to universal emotions and not controversial stories. A court case that is unresolved would, of course, not involve any emotion in the delivery. Universal emotions refer to emotions that all of us feel. This might apply to a story about children suffering or a family being killed in a fire.

Even what may appear to be a routine statement often sounds more effective if it reflects some emotion. Consider the line, "We'll continue hourly updates on the progression of the hurricane throughout the evening." For a listener sitting in a beach house in the path of this hurricane this is a very emotion-laden statement. Delivering this statement with a sense of concern would project the feeling that this station cares about its listeners.

Emotions run the gamut from joyful to tragic, happy to sad. It is important to analyze carefully the emotion of each story. There is a difference between a fire story where no one was killed, for example, and one with deaths. They are both serious, but the first is somber or grave, and the second is tragic or sad.

It is helpful to write the emotion of the story in the margin on the copy as a reminder. McCoy suggests you can even use "smiley" faces for upbeat sections and frowns for more serious paragraphs.

Stories may change emotion as they progress. Careful analysis is the only way to trace the progression of emotions. Listening to news headlines illustrates this. The first headline might deal with a tragic plane crash, followed by a frustrating traffic tie-up, and finishing with a joyful lottery winner headline. The anchor reading this would need to reflect these changes vocally.

There are some techniques that will help integrate emotion into delivery. You can precede your countdown with a phrase like, "Jim, I have a really sad story to tell you. Three, two, one. . . ." This will help capture the emotion before voicing.

If you find it is really difficult for you to portray any emotion with your voice, try reading children's stories out loud. Really exaggerate the emotion. Better yet, read to a child. The child will let you know right away if you are not reading with enough emotion.

You can practice with news copy as well. Let yourself laugh in a happy story and sound overly distraught in a sad one. This is for practice only, but it will help you push the parameters of what you can do with your voice in terms of emotion. You will want to pull back from the exaggeration in your on-air delivery.

Using emotion can add a human quality to delivery, but remember that it needs to be a sincere, universal emotion. Faking emotion or editorializing with your delivery is never appropriate.

Taking a few minutes to go through your copy and think about your listener and emotion before voicing can help create a sense of interpersonal communication with the listener. If you know to whom you are talking and can bring that person to life in your mind, you can reach out to that listener.

In television today the best broadcasters are not necessarily the ones with the booming, deep voices like the actor James Earl Jones or Ted Baxter, the TV anchor from "The Mary Tyler Moore Show." The best newscasters are the ones who communicate with their listeners. By marking your script and focusing on the person to whom you are talking, you can become a comfortable communicator on television.

Tips
Connecting with the listener in a very human way will build your credibility. Television and the Internet create very intimate human encounters even though they are through a monitor. Thinking of a real person will help you connect.

Practice
When talking on the telephone, use your imagination to create the visual image of the person to whom you're talking and really see the room where that person is. This will allow every telephone conversation to work as a

practice session. Likewise, when taping a message for your answer machine, see a real person in your mind.

Key Points

- Broadcasting is a human communication encounter with your listener.
- You will build your credibility if you connect with your listener and not just with the camera.
- Thinking of a real person will help you connect.
- Putting a person or people in a room where they are watching you will help.
- Marking your script will allow you to know where to breathe and which words to stress.

TIPS FOR BUSINESS

Once you have considered the verbal and nonverbal aspects of going on camera, and the opportunities available, you may decide you want to pursue a career in broadcasting. Many students and business people have no idea of how to get started working in the TV business. They have worked at honing their skills but do not know how to market themselves. The approach to marketing yourself in TV news is similar to TV commercials, industrials or soap operas.

Marketing Yourself

Whether you are pursuing news or commercials, you should start off marketing *yourself* before you seek to be represented by agencies or an agent. Even though you will have to become your own promotion person, you can be well respected in the business. In addition, you can keep your entire paycheck since you will not have to pay an agent's commission. The downside is that you will have to make a small, initial investment in marketing materials. If you are not a self-starter, this process will not be for you. The first item on your list will be a resume.

Resume

We have provided sample resumes for both prospective news practitioners (see Figure 22) and commercial spokespeople (see Figure 23). Understand that the reactions to your resume will be very subjective. Take a sample to several local news directors or producers at TV production houses for their review before distributing copies. (Who knows? You may impress one enough to get a job!). Once you have some feedback, you can finalize your copy with any necessary revisions.

Cover Letters

Many news directors, like Dave Cupp at WVIR in Charlottesville, Virginia, feel that the cover letter is the most important marketing tool you have. It shows your writing ability and how you can sell yourself. Cupp also points out that there is one thing he is always looking for first in your letter or your resume tape— it is not a good voice or good writing. He is looking for a reason *not* to hire you. With hundreds of tapes, resumes and cover letters to evaluate for each job opening, he has to find a reason not to hire 99 percent of the applicants. Do not let a sloppy cover letter be that reason.

Figure 22
Sample Entry-Level News Resume

Michelle Collins   65 Etchwood
                                                Chicago, Illinois
                                                (111) 111-1111

Broadcast Experience:

    KVVV 35 San Francisco, CA, 1999 to present
    News Desk Assistant for morning and midday

    WXYG, Atlanta, GA, 1997 to 1998
    Intern in Investigative Reporting Unit

    WMMM Macon, GA, 1996 to 1999
    Anchor for evening college newscast

    WMMM Macon, GA, 1995
    Field Reporter

Education:

    Merryman College: Macon Georgia
    Bachelor of Science in Broadcast News/2000

Professional Organizations

    Society of Professional Journalists
    Radio-Television News Directors Association

References

    Enclosed

Figure 23
Sample Commercial Spokesperson Resume

MICHELLE COLLINS
1111 Park Street
NY, New York 22113
(222) 100-0000

Hair: Brown
Eyes: Blue
Ht: 5'6

Commercials

Baby Talk, 2000
Walls Design, 2000
Shoe Palace, 1998
Tappan Square, 1998

Industrials

M & M Molding, 1999
Acme Surplus, 1999
Gem Jewels, 1998

Voice-Overs

Basker Bagels, 2000
Rippin Fabrics, 2000
Shoes-n-Stuff, 1999

Stage

Maria, *West Side Story*, Blossom Players, 1997

Film

Extra, *Sing Loud,* Jester Films, 2000

Education

BA, Theatre, Ripley College of Arts, 1996

Hobbies

Racquet Ball/Reading/Yoga/Traveling

Cupp also is adamant that if his ad says no calls—that means NO CALLS! News directors are very busy people with very little time allotted for hiring people. Phone calls that interrupt them can be very annoying and can cost you the job.

Here is more information Cupp offers that will help you in your job search:

Sending Yourself Through The Mail To A News Director
David Cupp, News Director
WVIR-TV, Charlottesville, Virginia

What would you say if I could promise you five minutes of the time of a news director who was hiring for a job you wanted to have? What would you say to convince him or her to give you a full-blown interview?

It might be tough to come up with a convincing argument, but my guess is you would *not* choose to simply hand that news director your materials and then stand mute for five minutes, remaining silent until he or she nodded and showed you out the door. Yet, figuratively speaking, that is precisely the choice most job applicants make every day when they pass up the opportunity to include personal letters when they send off their application materials.

When you are applying for a job I have listed, in essence you are sending yourself through the mail to me. Your resume shows me what your education and experience have been so far. Your tape shows me what you can do right now in front of a camera. A good letter can tell me even more than either of those. A good letter can give me a feel for what kind of person you are. It can tell me why you want to be in this business. It can show me how comfortable you are working with words and telling stories. It can convince me that out of the hundred or so applicants I am considering, you are one of the few I should bring in for an interview.

I think letters are so important I ask for them in every ad I place. But many applicants still fail to send them. Others dash off a few thoughtless, worthless sentences— a minimum response to my request. Only a few really take advantage of the opportunity I am offering, and those few are more likely to land interviews. An impressive letter can do you a lot of good, but remember that a lousy letter will kill your application outright. Indeed, sloppiness in any aspect of your application can kill your chance of landing a job.

With each new application I consider the first question I have to answer is simple: is this person better than, or at least as good as, the best I've seen so far? If the answer is no, I punch the eject button and move on. If the answer is yes . . . if I see something intriguing in your tape, something impressive in your resume, or something compelling in your letter . . . I will stay with you and I will want to know more.

Letters

- **Who are you?** What makes you tick? Why do you want to go into broadcast journalism? This is your chance to tell me.
- **Why do you want to work here?** Why this city? Why this station? Visit our web site and do some basic research if you don't already have an answer for this question.
- **Why should I hire you?** That's the last question I ask in my interviews, and I pay a lot of attention to the answers I get.
- **Sell your professionalism.** Tell me more about your skills and experience.
- **Explain your strengths.** Cite examples. What you've done is more important than what you say.

- **Don't boast.** Easy confidence is what you want to project.
- **Keep it simple and conversational.** As your news stories should be.
- **Always personalize.** "Dear News Director" is a strike against you.
- **Always proofread.** It's not enough to know my name. Find out how to spell it. My last name only has four letters. Cupp. But I've received letters addressed to Culp, Copp, Cup, Cupt, Kupp, and Tupp. Our call letters are WVIR-TV. But I've received letters addressed to WVIN, WIVR and KVIR. If you don't get my name or my call letters right, why should I expect you to be careful about details in your news stories, and why on earth should I hire you?

Spot The Blunders

Understand something crucial. This is a business in which lawsuits can hinge on misused words. Never, I repeat *never*, use a word in an application letter (or a news story) unless you know what it means and how it is spelled. Below is a list of real-life grammatical stumbles that have damaged or destroyed applicants' hiring prospects:

- Dear Perspective Employer:
- I'm a writer trying to brake into broadcasting.
- I am sorry the tape I sent earlier didn't work. I hope this copy fairs better.
- Dedication, determination, dependability. These adjectives should describe your next reporter.
- So I here that you are looking for a sports reporter with some "fresh ideas".
- If your looking for a sports reporter who is very versatile, I am your man!
- Please except this resume and tape as my application for the position.

- I'm writing with much interest in the job's currently open at WVIR-TV.
- I have the ability to employ traditional principals of journalism.
- I have made a strong effort to compliment my education with practical experience.
- I like the Old Dominion state very much and would like to work and live their again.

In addition, here are some quick tips related to your resume and your tape. First, heed this word of warning. News directors tend to be a contrary lot. Many would argue against some of the tips I'm about to give you. So use your own best judgment and remember these are not rules, just guidelines.

Resume Tips

- **Keep it short and simple.** Limit yourself to one page, two at the most, until you've been working in the business for several years.
- **Use quality bond paper.** Don't send cheap photocopies of your resume. You want it to look professional.
- **Make it attractive and easy to read.** I should be able to scan it in 15 seconds and get a thumbnail feel for your qualifications.
- **Lead with experience, including internships.** Real-life newsroom experience could help set you apart from the crowd. Follow with your education and training.
- **Don't explain the obvious.** Don't waste precious space explaining generic job responsibilities you carried out as a production assistant.
- **Do explain specific job skills you have.** Do you know how to shoot and edit videotape? How much of that have you done? Do you know how to run an Avid or a live truck? These are things I need to know, and far too many applicants leave me in the dark about them.
- **List awards and honors if impressive.** Were you on

the Dean's List? Did you graduate cum laude? Did you have a GPA above 3.5? Were you elected to any student offices?

- **Exclude "objective."** It's usually obvious. If you want to explain your objective, do so in your letter instead.
- **Include references and their phone numbers.** List several, and be sure all the information is accurate. I won't bother them unless I am interested in you, and if I am interested in you I may want to contact one or two of them first. "References Available Upon Request" creates extra work for me.

Resume Tape Tips

- **Format.** VHS is safe. Other than that, if it is not specified in the ad, call and ask, because technology changes so quickly.
- **Length.** Five to 15 minutes will be fine. I don't have time to watch more, and may watch a lot less.
- **No bars and tone.** Those are for engineers, and have no place on an audition tape. Open the tape with a slate containing your name, address and phone number if you have access to the technology to do so. Otherwise, get right to the content.
- **No on-air bios.** Don't perch on the edge of a desk in front of a camera and chat with me. Unless you have the presentation skills of a professional actor, you won't be able to pull it off. You will look awkward, and you will do yourself more harm than good.
- **Open with a montage of standups?** Maybe. Some news directors hate them and think they are narcissistic, but they don't bother me. I find them useful for answering the basic questions of what you look and sound like. If you don't open with a montage, be sure your first story includes a standup.
- **Lead with your best story**. Put your best work, whatever it is, up front. Follow with variety. A hard news story plus a feature plus a live shot would cover all

your bases well. Some news directors would tell you not to put any anchoring on your tape for an entry-level position. I don't agree. Many of my entry-level reporters wind up doing substitute anchoring within a matter of months. If you have an anchoring sample, I'd like to see it.

- **Label everything.** Tape and box. Face and at least one edge. Your tape will be put in a stack. Put your name on at least one edge where I can see it.
- **Put your rundown on a separate card.** Tape it to the inside of the box lid if you like, but don't make it part of the tape label. That would keep me from reading it while the tape was in the machine.

How To Get Started, by David Cupp

I'd like to share with you a few opening paragraphs from actual application letters and my reactions to them. They represent a variety of approaches and have nothing in common except that I had a strong response to each of them. Some I hated. Others I admired.

I am desirous of the opportunity of ascertaining a position within your sports department.

Huh? When I read this I hoped this guy was joking. He wasn't.

Dear News Director:
Hello, my name is _____ and first of all I'd be more personal but that's all you gave me on Media Line. That aside, you can obviously tell I'm looking for another job. I've been working for _____ for the past 18 months and feel its time to move on to bigger and better things.

I took an instant dislike to this guy one sentence into his letter. He appears to just be looking to get his ticket punched, and I didn't even bother to play his tape.

Who is Bruce Lindsay and why is he important to me? Who is Jackie Smith and how did he affect the outcome of the 1979 Super Bowl? What are M1, M2 and M3 and why are they relevant? Why do you and I care about these questions? The answer to the last question: because we are in television news . . . or at least you are. I am a television news wannabe and I am writing to you because I can bring versatility, knowledge and energy to your newsroom as a writer and/or producer.

Giving a pop quiz to your prospective employer is a high-risk approach, but this applicant's intelligence and audacity impressed me.

Before you toss this letter in a growing pile of resumes and tapes, let me tell you what you WON'T find in this EVENING ANCHOR candidate.
Not a clueless beauty queen trying to break into TV News.
Not a "green" journalist from Small Town, USA looking for her first job.
And, most importantly, not a "hot property" with an agent to match.
However, what you WILL find is a native Virginian who has gone away to Ohio and acquired lots of experience, and desires to come back to her home state.

This applicant has an effective writing style, and manages to convey a lot of information in a very small space.

This summer, I investigated developments of the independent press in the Eastern Bloc. Funded by a $7,000 travel grant, I hit 13 countries in 54 days—all without hotel reservations.

If I can survive that, I can do anything.

How about hiring me as a reporter?

This letter illustrates an extremely important point: All Life Experiences Are Transferable. I agree with this applicant's logic. If this guy did the things he listed at the top of his letter, he could likely handle any challenges a job in my newsroom might throw at him.

But you don't have to have European investigative experience to make the same argument. During a recent interview I noted that the applicant had worked as a waitress. She replied: "Yes, and I thought about taking that off my resume, but I left it in because I decided it showed that I could handle a job that involved physical challenges and deadline pressure while keeping a smile on my face and being charming." Having once worked as a waiter, I agree with her totally. And her rationale provides a perfect example of how you can make a case for your own hiring citing what you've learned from your own life experiences, even from menial jobs that would appear to have nothing to do with broadcasting.

Who says TV news is glamorous? Here's what I learned in journalism school: never wear high heels; an eight-hour day means it's only half over; and McDonald's wrappers are an excellent surface for drafting a script on the run. Of course, these lessons were secondary to learning about ethics, reporting and producing. But as a graduate student at _____, I honed my skills on the street and in the newsroom, not the classroom.

Earlier I mentioned "easy confidence" as the best tone to strike in an application letter. This is a good example of that.

When I used to play the game "Life," I never liked landing on the journalist or professor space at the beginning because it usually meant ending the game with the least amount of cash. After all, the doctor or lawyer spaces guaranteed a healthy income, which provided for more opportunities during the game. It is so ironic that the professions I claimed to disdain in my childhood days are the very ones I would like to call my life's work.

Before I become a history professor—I would like to be a journalist. I want to cover the stories that someday will inspire my students during a lecture. And I want to begin my journalistic experience here at Channel 29.

This was written by one of our interns, who was applying for a reporting job. I hired her, and her stories were as well-written as this letter was. She went on to become one of our primary anchors. She was also one of the best employees I ever had, and I believe you can get a sense of all that potential in reading this letter.

Agents

Before considering an agent, write down what you can tolerate and what you cannot. Stand firm when approaching an agent. Let the agent know your terms and conditions. For example, you may have to tell your prospective agent that you have a significant other, and that it is impossible for you to maintain a long-distance relationship. Clearly, you may scare some agents away if you have no flexibility, but this is your life, not theirs.

Utterback's *Broadcaster's Survival Guide* is an excellent resource to help you balance your life in the TV business.

Washington-based correspondent for CBS News Sharyl Attkisson suggests having a list of questions ready to ask when you meet any prospective agent.[1] Some questions are:

1. Are you a licensed agent?
2. Are you affiliated with a union like AFTRA?
3. What services do you provide?
4. Who are some of the clients you work with?
5. May I speak with some of your clients?

Agencies

You will discover that many people in commercials and industrials prefer agencies as opposed to one exclusive agent. An agency is a company, usually with more than one employee, that handles booking talent for auditions or jobs. One reason for you to consider working for an agency is that many producers will come to a city and call a prestigious agency when they need to cast a commercial or a film. Many professionals say it is more realistic to start out in the business with an agency rather than an agent. The reason is that agents will look for established performers so they can take a percentage of a higher income.

You still are faced with a percentage cut, however, if you decide to work for an agency. Watch out for agencies that require a start-up fee. This request is a clear indication that an agency is not legitimate. Agencies listed in your local AFTRA handbook are likely to be more trustworthy. Remember that signing with an agency or an agent is a two-way agreement. They have a right to reject you and you may bow out gracefully before signing anything.

The next step up from signing with an agent or an agency would be contracting with a personal manager. This person can manage everything from your career to your finances. According to Elaine Beardsley, author on TV commercials, the downside with managers is that you are relinquishing sometimes as much as 25 percent of your earnings.[2] You may notice that managers are very popular with sports celebrities. Your income should really be sizable if you are considering a manager.

Contracts

When you are working with an agent, always take a contract to a lawyer for review before signing. You also may change some of the language to fit your conditions and have the agent or agency sign off on your revisions. If you cannot come to an agreement with your prospective employer, chances are you do not want to work there. Keep plenty of copies of your contract in a safe place. TV news contracts vary, but the average contract lasts about two years. *Non-compete clauses* also are included in many contracts. These limit your option to take a new job in the same TV market for three months or more after your current contract expires or you resign from the position.

Exclusive contracts mean that you cannot work for any other agency or TV station during your tenure as an employee unless you have written consent. For example, if you work for X Talent Agency, you would not be able to take a job offered by Y Talent Agency. In addition, some phone calls for jobs come directly to you from TV production houses. You should discuss what is protocol with your agent or agency about accepting job offers that come to you. Agencies dislike this tactic because they prefer TV production companies and other constituents to call them directly, not you. Again, discuss these legalities with your lawyer so that you are clear about your commitment.

Unions

Unless you are looking for a job as news talent, you might also consider joining a union like AFTRA or the Screen Actors Guild (SAG). But prepare yourself for some confusion. It seems as if the AFTRA and SAG rules and rates change constantly. The best course to follow is to call your local chapter and ask if you can pay them a visit. You will get a handbook, and someone usually is kind enough to explain the details. You will discover that some of the performers' unions are sister unions. So if you are a member of one, it is easier to become a member of another. If you are pursuing TV performing as a full-time career, it pays to be in a union because you will be protected to some extent and have benefits available to you. Do not join the unions, however, until you are ready. Start-up registration fees and dues are very expensive, and joining a union does not guarantee you will get a job. For this reason, it may be better to begin your career as non-union talent.

Photos

If you plan to be a television performer and not a newscaster, the next item you should get is an 8x10 black-and-white photo taken that you can attach to the back of your resume. Producers, especially, like this approach because there is less chance of losing your materials. Many agency directors recommend that beginning talent create a list of photographers in the local area. You should visit these studios to examine the photographers' work and to get a price estimate. There is no better way to tell how proficient people are in their craft than seeing the product firsthand.

Once you have selected a photographer, you should schedule a shooting day. If you have never experienced a photo shoot, ask the photographer if you can sit in on a session. Also, get to know your photographer. The more comfortable you are, the better session you will have. This is where legitimate modeling schools like *Barbizon* can be very helpful because you will learn photo session techniques. What this all comes down to is what are you willing to invest. A question talent always have is whether to go with glossy or matte photos. While producers may have their preferences, it really does not matter. Decisions are critical, however, if you decide to create a composite photo.

A composite is a picture card with two or more photographs of you, sometimes on both sides. Often, you will find print models using composites, but it is not uncommon for people doing commercials for television to use them as well. For example, if you want to portray several characters, and you have not had the opportunity to cut a commercial or an industrial where you can incorporate them, a composite can show a producer what you would look like in various roles.

Demo Tape

If you are serious about a career in broadcasting, nothing is more important than a good demo tape. We will not attempt to teach you how to put together a demo tape, but there are books dedicated to this subject alone. Authors Susan and Larry Benedict explain that a demo tape is like a commercial, but the difference is *you* are the product.[3] This is true for TV news and for commercial TV. Do not be surprised if you hear the term "demo reel"—this is a throwback to the old days of radio when recordings were on reel-to-reel tapes. Demo reel means demo tape, or it may be referred to simply as your "reel." The advantage of a demo tape for TV is that news directors and producers can take a look at you while also assessing your sound.

Many corporate professionals who have appeared on video get "bit" by the bug to pursue TV commercials as supplementary work or to go into news. Are there coaches available to help you put a tape together? The answer is yes and no. Colleges can acquaint you with some great instructors, but make sure they are somehow currently working in news or commercials. Protocol seems to change in this business from year to year. If your interest is in news, simply call or e-mail a local station and ask if the news director or a producer can show you a demo tape. Most people are flattered when you ask them, but be courteous about their time. Here is a quick formula to use if you want to put together a demo tape for news or commercials:

Success Formula

1. *Decide* if you want to pursue TV news or commercial TV (commercials, industrials or acting). Never mix news and commercial TV on a demo tape. Keep a consistent look throughout your demo tape. Do not vary your hairstyle greatly or your wardrobe. News directors want to know what they are getting.

2. If you want to put a commercial tape together and you have never done a commercial or an industrial, you will have to come up with your own scripts, videographer, props, etc. This is difficult if you do not know anyone in the business, but most video production houses or agencies offer these services. Decide what is in your price range. If you are interested in news, video production houses also can work with you, but make sure you are coached by someone with experience in news. If you already have video footage, the next step is working with an editor.

3. *Editing* can get expensive. Shop around for good prices and an editor's good reputation when it comes to video production houses and editing services. While someone can guide you, always think of putting the best samples first and having a short tape. A casting agent for an

infomercial told McCoy that someone once sent in a demo tape with three industrials that lasted one hour. Clearly, producers do not have that kind of time when they are faced with looking at 30 tapes! Always, get a critique from a few professionals in the business before you start sending out tapes.

4. *Duplication* is the next item. Once your tape is ready, make sure you have labels printed with your name, address and phone number. Label the tape and tape box. (But always play back the tape in order to proof the duplication.) Tape duplication (dub) houses can create multiple copies of your tape for a more reasonable cost than a production house.

5. You are now ready to *mail* your tape, photo, cover letter and resume. Bubble-wrap envelopes are preferable to serve as protection for your tape. Label, label, label! Your tape may become separated from the packaging box, so label everything. On the tape box, include a rundown of what is on the tape in the event a news director wants to fast forward to a particular section. Mailing lists are available from professional organizations or the phone book. For commercial television, TV stations, video production houses, ad agencies and PR firms are great places to start with a mailing. Remember that PR and ad firms need talent in their clients' videos.

6. *Follow-up* is the last step before getting an audition or the job! Founder of Television Workshop, Inc., Gene Fallon, suggests you keep a correspondence log.[4] You need the contact's name, address and phone number, along with the dates you communicated and what was said. A monthly file is good when starting out. For example, you can record that you

called producer Sue Jones of Y Videos. Let us say that Sue received your video and liked it, but does not need your services just yet. Ask her if it would be acceptable to contact her on a monthly basis just to check in. This process is repeated over again many times, requiring you to be your own secretary. If you fail to provide enough details, chances are you will not recall the particulars that could help you develop a good rapport with a producer. Fallon advises that you can always alternate a monthly phone call with a card or some interesting marketing tactic.[5] This approach can prevent you from becoming a pest on the phone. National commercial spokesperson Jan Jones said, "It is good to become a *pleasant* pest in this business."

Audition Tips for Commercial Television

If you get an audition, there are some simple, general rules to follow:

1. Get the exact time and location of the audition and plan to arrive 10 minutes prior to your call. Always allow for extra drive time in case of traffic or road construction. Carry a cell phone so you can notify someone if you will be late. Take the phone number with you.
2. Ask if you should bring any materials and, for acting auditions, what should you wear.
3. Find out what you will be doing and whether it is possible to get a script in advance.
4. When you arrive at the audition, get your side or a script and focus on the copy, away from

other candidates. Mingling with others can distract and intimidate you. Mark your script accordingly.

5. Once your audition is concluded, thank the producer and follow up with a thank-you letter or card.

Interview and Audition Tips for News

Follow the same preparation steps regarding location and time from the previous list for commercial spokespeople.

1. Know the names of the news director and others you will meet.

2. Research the city and the state so that you can talk intelligently about the main news events. Also, study the station's web site thoroughly to get a good feel for the place, the people and the product.

3. Prepare two or three short story ideas to discuss.

4. Ask for a few minutes to read over and mark your script if you are doing an anchor audition.

5. If you can get a taped copy of a newscast from the station at which you are auditioning, you may develop a sense of what the news director is looking for, especially if you are not familiar with the co-anchor's delivery, etc.

Tips

For a commercial tape, be as creative as you can when you are corresponding. McCoy once sent some M&M candies to a producer, along with a business card, as a fun reminder that she was available for voice-over work. Producers really notice your creativity and will remember you when the next job is open. Note: If you are pursuing news, this practice may be perceived in a negative way.

Practice

Put together a "rough" portfolio of your work. Upgrade your resume, collect your tapes or create new ones, get a photo taken and have someone evaluate your package. What do you need to work on?

Key Points

- Decide on whether you need an agent or an agency to help market yourself. Keep in mind the percentage that will be taken from your income. Always work with someone who makes you feel comfortable and with whom you have good rapport.
- Before you sign a contract, make sure you review it with your lawyer so you know what you are getting into.
- Marketing yourself without an agent has many advantages, but the key is to be organized and willing to follow up with your prospects. Also, you have to be willing to make an initial investment in supplies.
- If you are interested in AFTRA or SAG

unions, call the chapter nearest you to find out all the details.

- Photos and resumes go hand in hand for commercial tapes. If you are starting out, consider an 8x10 black-and-white photo, along with your resume. Always have someone else give you feedback before distributing anything.
- Demo tapes essentially are commercials of you. Work with a good production company to get the tape assembled. News directors and producers like versatility on tapes but also prefer short tapes.
- Duplication of your tape is a must regardless of who is marketing you. Make sure your packaging is professional. Be sure all names are spelled correctly. If you are marketing yourself, keep good records in your follow-up correspondence with producers or news directors.
- If you get called for an audition, remember to be on time, come prepared and ask questions. If you are auditioning for commercial television, do not mingle with other talent before the audition—keep to yourself and stay focused.
- Cover letters and resumes represent you to someone you have not met. Make a good first impression. Check your spelling and your grammar, and have someone proof your documents. Call and get the correct spelling and title of the person you are contacting.

Good Luck!

NOTES

Chapter 1

1 Roger Fidler, *Mediamorphosis: Understanding New Media* (Thousand Oaks, California, Pine Forge Press, 1997) 25.

Chapter 3

1 Ann S. Utterback, *Broadcast Voice Handbook*: *How to Polish Your On-Air Delivery* (Chicago: Bonus Books, 2000).
2 Ibid.

Chapter 4

1 William L. Hagerman, *Broadcast Announcing* (Englewood Cliffs, NJ: Prentice Hall, 1993).

2 Ibid., 194.

3 Ibid.

4 Ibid.

5 Michael Patton, *Qualitative Evaluation Methods* (Beverly Hills, CA: Sage Publications, 1980).

Chapter 6

1 James Wilson and Stan Le Roy Wilson, Ph.D., *Mass Media Mass Culture: An Introduction* (New York: McGraw-Hill, 1998).

2 Squire Fridell, *Acting in Television Commercials for Fun and Profit* (New York, NY: Harmony Books, 1986) 126, 129.

3 Susan Blu and Molly Ann Mullin, *Word of Mouth: A Guide to Commercial Voice-Over Excellence* (Los Angeles, CA: Pomegranate Press, 1987).

Chapter 7

1 Douglas P. Brush and Judith M. Brush, *Private Television and Communications: Into the Eighties; The Third Brush Report* (LaGrangeville, NY: HI Press, Inc. 1981) 15.

2 Dale Young, *Prompt Ear*, (216) 221-0085.

3 Robert J. Samuelson, "The Internet and Gutenberg," *Newsweek*, January 24, 2000.

Chapter 8

1 Edwin Wilson, *The Theater Experience* (NY: McGraw-Hill, 1994).

2 Ibid., 110-115.

3 Marsh Cassady, *The Theatre and You: A Beginning* (Colorado Springs, Colorado: Meriwether, 1992) 200.

4 Michael Caine, *Acting in Film: A 60-Minute Master Class with Michael Caine* (Dramatis Personae, BBC Production, Applause Acting Series, 1990).

Chapter 9

1 James Wilson and Stan Le Roy Wilson, Ph.D., *Mass Media Mass Culture: An Introduction* (New York: McGraw-Hill, 1998) 285-286.

Chapter 11

1 Dawn Waldrop, *Best Impressions*: *How to Gain Professionalism, Promotion and Profit* (Cleveland, OH: BookMasters, Inc. 1997).

2 John Rosenbaum and Alan Wurtzel, *Television Production* (New York: McGraw-Hill,1995) 501.

3 *Barbizon Models Handbook* (NY: Barbizon International, Inc.) Note: Available only through independent Barbizon franchises.

Chapter 14

1 Sharyl Attkisson, *So You Want an Agent?* (New York: Self-Published Booklet, 1997) 18,19.

2 Elaine Keller Beardsley, *Working in Commercials: A Complete Sourcebook for Adult and Child Actors* (Boston, MA: Focal Press, 1993).

3 Larry and Susan Benedict, *The Video Demo Tape*: *How to Make a Tape that Gets You Work* (Boston, MA: Focal Press, 1992).

4 Gene Fallon, *Television Workshop: Freelance Starter Kit* (Cleveland, OH: Television Workshop, Inc., 1982).

5 Ibid.

GLOSSARY

Accessories—Items used to enhance a wardrobe.

Acrylic Nails—Artificial nails that are made with acrylic material.

Aesthetic Director—A person who works exclusively with talent during a production, similar to a theatre director.

AFTRA—American Federation of Television and Radio Artists. This is the union for TV spokespeople.

Air Checks—A procedure in which talent view their recorded material to see if they are satisfied with the quality of their work. Also, some producers use this term if they are checking audio levels or the quality of the picture.

Alpha Hydroxy—An acid-based lotion or cream that is applied to the face so that fine lines become diminished, creating more of a youthful appearance.

Anchor—A term used to refer to a TV spokesperson, usually in news.

Articulators—The lips, teeth, tongue and jaw, which are used to shape sound waves into phonemes.

Backdrop—A material used as a set piece.

Base—A term used for makeup foundation.

BIO—A term used in place of a resume for talent.

Blocking—A term used to designate movement in a film or TV scene.

Bloom—A term used when objects tend to glow on TV. This phenomenon usually is the result the camera's reaction to anything white being used or worn on a TV set.

Blush—A product usually applied to the face to create a sense of color.

Bob Cut—A hairstyle that was popularized by Jackie Kennedy, and worn by many TV anchors because of its conservative look.

Breath Support—The ability to take in a large volume of air and the ability to control the exhalation of that air.

Bridge—A segue that connects news stories.

B-Roll—Cut-away video footage that usually has no sound.

Camera—A device that processes an optical image into a video signal that can either be recorded or displayed on a TV monitor.

CD-ROM—A compact disk that features read-only memory.

Celebrity Spots—Spots that incorporate some kind of famous person to endorse the product.

Character Makeup—Basic, corrective makeup that is enhanced to create a specific character.

Character Spots—Commercials where identifiable characters are continually used.

Chroma-Key—A special effect that uses color as a replacement background for an inserted video source.

Closed-ended Question—A question that usually fosters a definitive, short answer, allowing for little expansion on the interviewee's part.

Collagen Injections—Injections people use to diminish lines on the face. Preferably, the procedure is performed by a dermatologist or a plastic surgeon.

Concealer—A cream applied to diminish dark circles under the eyes or any demarcations on the skin.

Consignment Shop—A store that sells mostly quality, second-hand clothing at very reasonable prices.

Consultant—Someone who is called upon to counsel or offer expert advice.

Control Room Director—A person who is in charge of the flow of a television production by calling the shots and controlling the technical aspects.

Corporate Video—Video intended to be used for a corporate, non-broadcast setting. Also referred to as "industrials."

Corporate Video Production House—A term used for a video production facility that specializes in corporate videos.

Corrective Makeup—A makeup approach used for talent who

want to come across as every-day people. The application is designed to look natural, enhancing the person's features.

Cosmetologist—An individual who is licensed to work as a hair stylist or makeup practitioner.

Crew—A group of people assembled to work on a video production.

Cue—A visual signal given to talent by the floor director.

Cue Cards—Cards that are used to prompt talent with lines from the script.

Demonstration Commercial—A spot that usually has talent demonstrating the product.

Demonstration Show—A TV show with a product or a service that is demonstrated for the viewing audience.

Denasality—Too little nasal resonance.

Diaphragm—Large sheet-like muscle that separates the thoracic cavity from the abdominal cavity and is used for breathing.

Diffusion—A material placed over lighting instruments that creates an indistinct light beam for the purpose of softening shadows.

Distance Learning—A teaching and learning situation in which the instructor and the learners are geographically separated and rely on electronic means for instructional delivery.

Donuts—A name for commercials that open with music, then go into copy and conclude with music.

Dry Run—A run through of a production without going live.

Dual Application—Makeup bases consisting of both a foundation and a powder.

Ear Assist—A device consisting of a tape recorder and an earpiece used to prompt talent with script lines.

Electronic Media—A term given to non-print forms of media. For example, radio, television, video and computer applications.

Esthetician—A licensed practitioner who specializes in skin-care procedures and makeup.

Facial—A procedure performed by a licensed practitioner who cleanses and refines the face.

Facial Peels—A peel-off facial application designed to exfoliate and hydrate the skin.

Filler Words—Unnecessary words used by talent to fill in pauses, such as "um."

Floor Director—A person responsible for all activities in the studio, such as visual/aural cues, talent assistance and location preparation.

Foundation—Another term for makeup base.

Gaffer Tape—A wide, sticky tape that has multiple uses in television, such as affixing microphone cables. Often called duct tape.

Gel Nails—An artificial nail that is developed with the use of ultraviolet light.

Gels—A color filter placed in front of lights to give the light beam a designated hue.

Gooseneck Microphone Stand—A flexible microphone stand that allows for better microphone adjustment.

Hand-Held Microphone—A microphone held by talent, as opposed to being on a stand. Usually used by talent for interview segments.

HDTV—An acronym for high definition television.

Heart-Shaped Face—A facial shape that is wide at the forehead and narrow at the cheeks. This person should avoid short styles.

Host—The principal spokesperson in a TV show, especially a talk show or an interview format.

IFB—Interruptible feedback. An earpiece used by talent so that TV directors can communicate with them in a live situation.

Industrials—Another name for corporate video.

Inflection—A change in pitch when speaking.

Infomercial—A TV program that sometimes mimics news and feature stories or a talk show, but really is a disguised commercial sales pitch for a product or a service.

In-House—A term used for a production facility that is within a corporation.

Jingle—Musical commercial themes, usually with a singer or a chorus.

Key Lights—The main source of illumination in a studio setting.

Lavalier Microphone—A small microphone that is attached to talent's clothing.

Live—A word used when a production is on air for the viewing audience to see in real time.

Live on Tape—This term is applied when a program is taped straight through, with very little editing.

Marks—A place marked where talent should stand or place props.

Mascara—A makeup product used to lengthen and enhance the eyelashes.

Matte—Term for dull, soft finish, as in makeup.

Meaning-Laden Words—The words that we must have to understand a news story.

Method Acting—An acting approach created by Russian actor Constantin Stanislavski.

Multimedia—The integrated computer display of motion and still images, sound and text.

Nasality—An excessive amount of nasal resonance, which produces the classic nasal voice.

Non-Commercial Video—Another term for industrial video.

Oblong-Shaped Face—A facial shape that resembles a vertical rectangle. Avoid long hairstyles.

Oil-Based Makeup—A makeup with oil blended into the product. Water is not a component in this product. Coverage is excellent, but powder must be applied on top of the application because of the greasy consistency.

On-Camera Commercial—When talent appear on camera for a commercial, as opposed to a voice-over.

On-Location—A video production done outside of a studio setting.

Oval-Shaped Face—Considered the ideal shape because the facial bones are in proportion. A person with an oval face can wear any hair style.

Package—A taped story done by a television news reporter. It usually includes a bridge or a stand-up. Most of the package is voice-over video.

Pancake Makeup—Makeup that comes in a powder cake. The cake must be moistened with water and applied with a sponge to the face. This makeup is excellent for balding men because of its matte finish.

Performance Director—A person who works with and guides talent during a production.

Phonation—Occurs when the air from the lungs is altered to create sound waves.

Phonemes—Individual sounds that combine to create words.

Plain Folks Commercial—A type of commercial that uses everyday, non-intimidating people as spokespeople.

Press Conference—A gathering held for the press to get information and updates about a specific event or person, usually presented by a spokesperson.

Product Commercials—A commercial sometimes involving talent, but usually focusing on the product, without a script.

Production—In television, a production is the process of creating a video.

Production Director—A person who operates the video switcher board. Also, another name given to the control room director who works exclusively with the technical crew.

PSAs—Public service announcements. These voice-overs tend to be used for public awareness through non-profit organizations.

Ready Cue—A command given by the floor director to alert studio personnel to the beginning of a show or a segment. Also, a command given by the control room director to prepare each technical crew person during a production.

Realism Commercial—A term used for a commercial that reflects reality or a "slice of life."

Resonance—Occurs when sound waves are augmented and enriched as they pass through resonating cavities (the throat, the oral cavity and, at times, the nasal cavity).

Retin-A—A prescribed cream used on the face to diminish lines.

Rip-and-Read—Reading news material on the air for the first time cold with no read-through.

Round-Shaped Face—A facial shape that is wide in proportion to its features, especially in the cheekbone area. Shoulder-length hairstyles should detract from the roundness, creating the illusion of an oval face.

Shotgun Microphone—A microphone used to obtain audio from a distance.

Side—A portion of a film script.

Skin Peels—A cosmetic procedure that exfoliates the skin, creating a look that is more youthful.

Slate Board—A board used to identify different segments in film or television.

Sound Booth—A small recording studio room with excellent acoustics for talent.

Spots—Commercials.

Square-Shaped Face—A very severe facial shape. Hairstyles should be shoulder length, softly framing the face.

Stand By Cue—A command given by the floor director to quiet every person in the studio before a production.

Stand-Up—A live or taped sequence where a news reporter talks directly into the camera. This is called a bridge if it is within a package and a stand-up close if it is at the end.

Stance—Talent's facial position at the beginning or the end of segment, on location, or on a set.

Still Store—A service that digitally grabs, freezes and displays a video frame.

Studio—A room where TV productions take place, either live or taped.

Take—A term that refers to the number of times a scene is filmed or taped.

Talent—A spokesperson on camera.

Talent Agencies—Organizations designed to find jobs for talent.

Talking Points—Points talent should cover when doing live stand-ups.

Tally Lights—Bright red lights located on the front of a camera. They are used to show talent which camera is currently selected on the video switcher board.

Teleconference—A transmission of media over satellite, from one or various places to other points, used to replace a traditional conference or meeting.

TelePrompTer—An electronic device often used in the studio to prompt talent with script lines.

Testimonial—A commercial that tends to be very believable because the talent have used the products.

Vocal Folds or **Cords**—Two tiny pieces of muscle and ligament in your throat that produce sound waves when air passes through their closed valve.

Vocal Inflection—When the voice varies in pitch, allowing for an interesting sound as opposed to monotone.

Voice-Over—When talent are called on to voice (read) copy off-camera for a TV production.

Warm-Up—A period of time used for hosts of a talk show to debrief their interviewees, usually before the show begins.

Wireless Microphone—An audio device that allows the talent to move without the limitations of audio cables.

Witch Hazel—A product that can be used as an astringent for the face.

Wrap-Up—A signal or a term used for TV hosts to know when there is very little time left in a TV program, signaling for them to get ready to sign off.

SUGGESTED READINGS AND INFORMATION

Attkisson, Sharyl. *So. . . You Want an Agent?* New York, NY: Self-Published Booklet, 1997.

Barbizon Models Handbook. New York: Barbizon International, Inc. Note: Available only through independent Barbizon franchises, (504) 330-1111.

Beardsley, Elaine Keller. *Working in Commercials: A Complete Sourcebook for Adult and Child Actors.* Boston, MA: Focal Press, 1993.

Benedict, Larry and Benedict, Susan. *The Video Demo Tape That Gets You Work.* Boston, MA: Focal Press, 1992.

Blu, Susan and Mullin, Molly Ann. *Word of Mouth: A Guide to Commercial Voice-Over Excellence.* Los Angeles, CA: Pomegranate Press, 1987.

Cassady, Marsh. *The Theatre and You: A Beginning.* Colorado Springs, Colorado: Meriwether, 1992.

Fidler, Roger. *Mediamorphosis: Understanding New Media.* Thousand Oaks, CA: Pine Forge Press, 1997.

Fridell, Squire. *Acting in Commercials for Fun and Profit.* New York, NY: Harmony Books, 1986.

Hagerman, William L. *Broadcast Announcing.* Englewood Cliffs, NJ : Prentice Hall, 1993.

Mathis, Darlene. *Women of Color: The Muticultural Guide to Fashion and Beauty.* New York: Balantine Books, 1994.

Patton, Michael. *Qualitative Evaluation Methods.* Beverly Hills, CA: Sage Publications, 1980.

Utterback, Ann S. *Broadcaster's Survival Guide: Staying Alive in the Business.* Chicago, IL: Bonus Books Inc., 1997.

Utterback, Ann S. *Broadcast Voice Handbook: How to Polish Your On-Air Delivery.* Chicago, IL: Bonus Books Inc., 2000.

Waldrop, Dawn. *Best Impressions: How to Gain Professionalism Promotion and Profit.* Cleveland, OH: BookMasters, Inc., 1997.

Wurtzel, Alan & Rosenbaum, John. *Television Production.* New York: McGraw-Hill, 1995.

Wilson, Edwin. *The Theater Experience.* New York: McGraw-Hill, 1994.

Young, Dale: For more information on the *PromptEar*, call (216) 221-0085.

Index

A

Abdominal-diaphragmatic breathing, 133–35
Acting (film and TV)
  blocking and movement, 84
  energy maintenance, 85–86
  key points, 87
  memorization, listening, reacting, 82, 84
  props, 85
  script analysis, 81–82
  stage vs. TV and film, 80–81
  technique, 77–81
Actor, profile, 79–80
Aesthetic director, 8
Agencies, 168–69
Agents, 167–69
Air checks, 26
Alcohol, 93
Alpha hydroxy, 102
Alterations, wardrobe, 129
American Federation of Television and Radio Artists, 100, 110–11, 168, 179
Anchor, 21, 22, 25–26
  key points, 28–29
  movement and, 26
  spontaneity, 27–28
  stance, 27
  TelePrompTers and, 26
Anchors, 21, 22
Antihistamines, 138
Application letters, 164–67
Articulation, 140–42
Artz, Dr. Sheldon, 101–2
Attkisson, Sharyl, 168
Audio checks, 13, 16–17
Auditions, 54, 68, 72
Audition tips, 174–75

B

Baby wipes, 94
Backdrops, 119

Barbizon, 171
Base, 94–95
Basic Process, The, 57–58
Baxter, Ted, 152
Beaded material, 120
Beardsley, Elaine, 168–69
Belts, 122
Benedict, Susan and Larry, 171
Best Impressions, 113
Beverage drinking, 105
Blocking, 55, 84
Blu, Susan, 57
Blush, 95
Bob Evans Farms, 2
Body, 79
Body language, 25
Booking
    producer and, 32–33
    talk show guests, 43–44
Breathing, 132–35
Breath marks, 145
Breath support, 135
Brightness, 98
Broadcaster's Survival Guide, 86,
    168
Broadway shows, 84
B-roll, 111
Brushes, 95–96
Business tips, 155–77

C
Caffeine, 139
Caine, Michael, 80
Call-in-shows, 39–40
Camera set-up, 38
Caribbean, 65
CBS affiliate, 24
CBS News, 168
CD-ROM, 1, 74
Celebrity commercial, 52
Cell phone, 47
Character, 68
    spot, 52
    types, 53

Chiffon, 120–21
Classic style, 114
Clavicular breathing, 134
Clock out, 58
Clothing, 72
    textures, 119–21
CNN, 39, 63
College graduates, 3
Colors, 118
Commercial, 51–52
    auditions, 54
    character types, 53
    donut spot, 59–60
    key points, 61
    marks and props, 55
    on-camera, 56
    preparation, 54–55
    product display, 55–56
    script, 70
    shooting day, 56–57
    stance, 61
    timing, 58–59
    voice-overs, 57–58
Communication, 143–45
Composite, 171
Concealer, 94
Concentration, 78
Confirmation letter, 44
Content, industrial video, 67–68
Continuity person, 85
Contracts, 169
Control room director, 8, 13
Conversational presentation, 143–44
    emotion, 150–52
    key points, 153
    script marking, 144–48
    talking to a person, 149–50
Cosmetic surgery, 101–2
Cosmetology license, 111
Cotton, 121
Cotton balls, 93
Cotton swabs, 93
Coughing, 137
Cover letter, 156, 160–61
Cue cards, 11, 18, 65

Cues, 11–12, 13, 14–16
Cupp, Dave, 156, 159–64
Cusick, Mary, 2

D

Dairy products, 138
Delivery, industrial video, 67–68
Demonstrations, 40
Demonstrator, 52
Demo tape, 171–74
Denasality, 140
Department stores, 99–100
Desk microphone, 10
Diaphragm, 132–33
Diffusion, 98
Directors, 7–8
Discount store, 100
Distance learning, 73
Dominic, Virgil, 24
Donut spot, 59–60
Dramatic style, 115
Drug store, 100
Dry run, 73
Duplication, tape, 173

E

Ear assist, 65–67
Earrings, 127
Editing, tape, 172–73
Effects, 54
Electronic prompters, 11
Emotion, 150–52
Emotional recall, 78
Energy maintenance, 85–86
Environment, 65
Executives, prepared for broadcast-
    ing, 1–2
Eyebrow pencil, 96–97
Eyeglasses, 123
Eyeliner, 97
Eye moisturizer, 94
Eye movement, 11
Eye shadow, 96

F

Fabric blends, 121
Fabrics, 119–21
Face moisturizer, 94
Facial shapes, 108
Facial tissue, 94
Fact gathering, 33–34
Fallon, Gene, 173
Fear, 2–3
Fidler, Roger, 1
Filler words, 36–37, 49
Floor director, 11, 13, 48
Follow-up, 173–74
Follow-up questions, 36
Fridell, Squire, 51

G

Gaffer tape, 16
Gels, 98
Gooseneck, 10
Green room, 48
Group Theatre, The, 78
Guests, 32–33

H

Hagerman, William, 33, 36
Hairstyles, 3, 23, 107, 109
    consultations, 110–11
    facial shapes, 108
    key points, 112
    textures and products, 109–10
Hamlet, 81
Hand-held microphone, 9
Hand signals, 12, 13, 14–16
Hanson, Gary, 22
Headset microphone, 10
Healthy lifestyle, 3
Hearing Instrument Services, 65
High-definition television, 101
Hollywood, 52
Hoover Company, The, 54

I

IFB, 23, 27, 46
Industrial video, 63–64
 auditions, 68, 72
 character, 68
 clothing, 72
 content, delivery, 67–68
 distance learning, 73
 ear assist, 65–67
 environment, 65
 Internet and, 73–74
 key points, 75
 product, 64
 teleconferences, 73
Inner truth, 78
Internet, 34, 45, 73–74
 compared to television, 1–2
 industrial videos, 64
 types of broadcasts, 2
Interruptible feedback, 23
Interviews, 9
Inverted pyramid, 78–79

J

Jewelry, 16, 126, 127
Jingle, 59
Jones, James Earl, 152
Jones, Jan, 174

K

Kennedy, Jackie, 109
Kent State University, 74
Key lights, 98
King, Larry, 39

L

Lace, 120–21
La Mura, Mark, 81
Lavalier microphone, 8–9, 13, 16
Lighting, 98–99
Linen, 120
Liner, 96

Lipstick, 96
Listening, 82, 84
Live broadcasts, 9, 73
Live shots, 24

M

Mailing lists, 173
Makeup, 23, 45, 91–98
 aging and cosmetic surgery, 101–2
 application, 3
 application for men, 104
 application for women, 103
 consultant, 100
 key points, 105–6
 lighting and, 98–99
 people of color, 100–101
 remover (cleanser), 93
 shopping, 99–100
Marks, 55
"Mary Tyler Moore Show, The,"
 152
Mascara, 97
Mathis, Darlene, 100
Maurrant, Rose (character), 81
McCoy, Michelle, 37, 45, 58, 67, 79,
 86, 95, 98, 141, 148, 151, 173
McCoy, Tim, 3
Meaning-laden words, 146–48
Media training, xii
Memorization, 82, 84
Method approach, to acting, 78–79
Microphone, 8–10
 correct gripping of, 9–10
 dressing, 13, 16–17
Molrales, Olga, 94, 96
Moscow Art Theater, 78
Mouth breathing, 138
Movement, 84
Mullin, Molly Ann, 57
Multiple edits, 54
Multiple questions, 36
Murray, Gordon J., 74
Murrow, Edward R., 21
Musical performances, 9

N

Nails, 111
Nasality, 140
Natural style, 114–15
NBC television affiliate, 3
Necklaces, 127
News reporter, 21, 22
  interview and audition tips, 175–76
  job of, 22
  key points, 28–29
  live shots, 24
  movement and, 25
  preparation, 22–23
  talking points, 24
  writing, 25
News script, 69

O

Objectives, 79
Opportunities, 5
Outdoor lighting, 98–99

P

Patton, Michael, 38
PBS, 63
Performance director, 8
Personality, xi
Phonation, 136
Phonemes, 140
Photos, 170–71
Plain folks commercial, 52
Point of purchase videos, 63
Polyester/cotton blends, 121
Positions, on-air, 22
Posture, 13
Powder, 97–98
Powder puffs, 93
Prank call, 39–40
Preparation, 47, 54–55
Probing questions, 36
Producer, 7
Product, 55–56, 64
Production assistants, 17–18, 48

PromptEar, 65
Pronunciation, 64, 72, 144–45
Proofreading, 161–62
Props, 55, 85
Public Relations Society of America, 2
Public service announcements, 58
Punctuality, 47
Purell, 93

Q

Question guides, 34–35
Questions
  in advance, 45–46
  structuring, 35–38

R

Radio talk show, senior executives on, 1
Radio-Television News Director's Association, 22
Rayon, 121
Reacting, 82, 84
Ready cue, 11–12
Realism commercial, 52
Rehearsal, reading, 11
Relaxation, 78, 132
Remote settings, 9
Research, 32, 45–46
Resonance, 139–40
Resume, 3, 34, 156, 157, 158, 162–63
Resume tape, 163–64
Retin A, 101
Richie, Charles, 54
Romantic style, 115–16

S

Samuelson, Robert, 73
Satin, 120
Scarves, 122, 124–25
Screen Actors Guild, 170

Script
   analysis, 81–82
   commercial, 70
   hard news, 69
   industrial, 68, 71–72
   marking, 144–48
Self marketing, 155–56, 159–64
Sentence lead-ins, 36
Sequins, 120
Set, 46–47
Settings, 38–39
Shooting
   day, 56–57
   schedule, 85–86
Shopping, 128
Shotgun microphone, 9
Show time, 48–49
Side, 82
Silk, 120
Slate board, 85
Smoking, 137
Soap operas, 9
Sound booth, 10
Specific activities, 78
Spontaneity, 27–28
Spots. *See* Commercials
Stage acting, 80–81
Stance, 27
Standby cue, 11–12
Stanislavski, Constantin, 78–79, 80, 81
Station, 23
Still store, 73
Stipends, 44
Street Scene, 81
Stress reduction, 3
Studio, 7–8
   basics, 3
   cues, 11–12, 13, 14–16
   key points, 18–19
   microphones, 8–10
   recordings, 9
   TelePrompTers, 10–11
Supplies, 92

T
Tackle box, 93
Talking points, 24
Talk show
   call-in shows, 39–40
   demonstrations, 40
   experience, 24
   fact gathering, 33–34
   finding guests, 32–33
   key points, 40–41
   question guides, 34–35
   settings, 38–39
   structuring questions, 35–38
   topics, 31–32
   warm-ups, 39
Talk show guests
   appearance, 44–45
   booking, 43–44
   key points, 49–50
   preparation, 47
   research, 45–46
   set, 46–47
   show time, 48–49
Tally light change, 12
Technical director, 8
Teleconference, 1, 46, 73
TelePrompTer, 10–11, 26, 29, 54, 65, 66
Television acting, 3
Television talk show, senior executives on, 1
Television Workshop, Inc., 173
Testimonial commercial, 52
Theatrical makeup stores, 99
Thomas, Dave, 52
Thomas, Rhon, 82
Throat clearing, 137
Ties, 122, 127
Tongue twisters, 141
Toolbox, 89
Trailer, 86
Travel expenses, 44
TV monitors, 40
Tweed, 121
Two shot, 12

U

Unions, 170
Utterback, Ann S., 24, 26, 29, 48,
   68, 57, 86, 137, 147, 149, 168

V

Visualization, 149–50
Vocal delivery, standing for, 10
Vocal inflections, 3
Voice, 79, 131–32
   articulation, 140–42
   breathing, 132–35
   health, 136–39
   key points, 142
   level check, 16–17
   phonation, 136
   resonance, 139–40
Voice-overs, 3, 10, 51, 57–58

W

Waldrop, Dawn E., 113–14, 120,
   128, 129
Walters, Barbara, 36
Wardrobe, 65, 113–14
   accessories, 122–27

alterations, 129
backdrops, 119
colors, 118
fabrics, textures, 119–21
key points, 129–30
requirements, 3
selection, weather and, 22–23
shopping, 128
style, 114–16
things to remember, 117
Warm-up, 39, 48
Watches, 127
Websites, senior executives on, 1
Wendy's, 52
White House, 9
Wilson, Edwin, 78
Wilson, Stan LeRoy, 51
Wireless microphone, 10
Witch hazel, 93
Wrap-up question, 37
Writing, 25
WVIR, 156, 159

Y

Young, Dale, 65, 66

Remember to
Breathe!

"Ann Utterback is so much more than a voice coach. Working with her has not only made me better at my job, but she's helped me balance my career and my life outside of the newsroom."

Lauren Ashburn, reporter/anchor
WJLA-TV, Washington, D.C.

Would you like to work with Dr. Utterback to improve your voice and/or reduce your stress? Professional services include:

- Voice and Performance Telephone Tape Evaluations
- Telephone Stress Reduction Counseling
- Personal appointments in the Washington, D.C., Area
- On-Site Appointments, Workshops, and Lectures

For more information, contact Dr. Utterback
at her website: www.AVoiceDoc.com
or call 301-963-8463

"As a fledgling reporter, I thought I'd never sit behind an anchor desk because of my voice. Dr. Utterback showed me how to make the most of what I have through simple, reporter-friendly techniques."

Donya Archer, Co-anchor, WTXF-TV
Philadelphia, Pennsylvania

Also Available

Improve Your Delivery

BROADCASTER'S SURVIVAL GUIDE: STAYING ALIVE IN THE BUSINESS, first edition   **$24.95**

There is no profession more stressful than broadcasting. This book describes survival techniques to help everyone in broadcasting recognize stresses and deal with them in healthy ways. This is a self-help manual to use whenever stress is a problem for on-air staff, producers, writers, news directors, and anyone in the business. It's sure to be a guide that is referred to over and over.

BROADCAST VOICE HANDBOOK: HOW TO POLISH YOUR ON-AIR DELIVERY, third edition   **$39.95**

With over thirty years of experience in voice, Dr. Utterback knows what it takes to create and maintain an effective broadcast voice. This book teaches you how to find your best voice, and how to care for your voice so that it will last a lifetime. Earlier editions have been used in many newsrooms. They have also been widely adopted by such schools as the American University and the University of Missouri-Columbia.

THE UTTERBACK AUDIO TAPE SERIES

VOCAL EXERCISES   **$19.95**

Dr. Utterback leads you step-by-step through exercises and drills to improve breathing, increase resonance, and polish articulation.

VOCAL EXPRESSIVENESS   **$19.95**

Dr Utterback explains two methods to use to bring news stories to life: script marking and an interpersonal communication approach.

COPING WITH STRESS   **$19.95**

Dr. Utterback talks about stress—what it is, how it affects the body and the voice, and ways to begin to stress-proof your life.

RELAXATION PRACTICE   **$19.95**

This tape offers four different ten-minute relaxation periods that can be done in the office or at home.

Books and tapes are available from: **Bonus Books, Inc.**
phone: (312) 467-0580 *or call toll-free:* (800) 225-3775
fax: (312) 467-9271
www.bonus-books.com

Dr. Utterback is available for consultations by telephone or in her office. You will find more information at www.AVoiceDoc.com